The Politics of Discipleship
and Discipleship in Politics

The Politics of Discipleship and Discipleship in Politics

Jürgen Moltmann Lectures
in Dialogue with Mennonite Scholars

Jürgen Moltmann

Edited by Willard M. Swartley

Cascade Books
A division of *Wipf & Stock Publishers*
199 West 8th Avenue, Suite 3 • Eugene OR 97401

THE POLITICS OF DISCIPLESHIP AND DISCIPLESHIP IN POLITICS
Jürgen Moltmann Lectures in Dialogue with Mennonite Scholars

ISBN: 1-59752-483-2

Cataloging information:

Moltmann, Jürgen
    The politics of discipleship and discipleship in politics : Jürgen Moltmann lectures in
    dialogue with Mennonite scholars / Jürgen Moltmann et al.; edited by Willard Swartley.

    p.; cm.
    1. Moltmann, Jürgen. 2. Religion and Politics. 3. Peace—Religious Aspects—
    Christianity. I. Title. II. Swartley, Willard. III. Yoder, John Howard. IV. Finger, Thomas.
    V. Bauman, Clarence. VI. Harder, Helmut. VII. Friesen, LeRoy. VIII. Koontz, Ted. IX.
    Yoder, Perry.

    ISBN 1-59752-483-2

    BR115   M6413   2006

Manufactured in the U.S.A.

Contents

Acknowledgments

Moltmann's four lectures were first published as *Following Jesus Christ in the World Today: Responsibility for the World and Christian Discipleship*, *Occasional Papers* No. 4. Institute of Mennonite Studies (Elkhart, Indiana) and CMBC Publications (Winnipeg, Manitoba) 1983. Copyright 1983 Jürgen Moltmann.

The response articles were first published as *Dialogue Sequel to Jürgen Moltmann's Following Jesus Christ in the World Today*, *Occasional Papers* No. 8. Institute of Mennonite Studies (Elkhart, Indiana) and CMBC Publications (Winnipeg, Manitoba) 1984. Used by permission of the Institute of Mennonite Studies and CMU Press.

Jürgen Moltmann's essay "Peacemaking and Dragonslaying in Christianity" was translated by K. C. Hanson and Margaret Kohl. It first appeared as "Friedenstiften und Drachentöten in Christentum," *Evangelische Theologie* 64 (2004) 285–94. Used by permission.

Contributors

Clarence Bauman was Professor of Theology and Ethics (1928–95) at the Associated Mennonite Biblical Seminaries and the author of *The Sermon on the Mount: The Quest for Its Meaning* and *The Spiritual Legacy of Hans Denck*.

Thomas N. Finger was formerly Professor of Systematic and Spiritual Theology at Eastern Mennonite Seminary and is the author of *A Contemporary Anabaptist Theology; Self, Earth and Society* and *Christian Theology: An Eschatological Approach*.

LeRoy Friesen is the author of *Mennonite Witness in the Middle East: A Missiological Introduction*.

Helmut Harder is Professor of Theology Emeritus at Canadian Mennonite Bible College and the author of *Witnessing to Christ in Today's World* and *Guide to Faith*.

Ted Koontz is Professor of Ethics and Peace Studies and the Director of Peace and Justice Studies at Associated Mennonite Biblical Seminary. He is author of numerous articles on peace witness, two in *Mennonite Quarterly Review* (1995, 2003).

Marlin E. Miller (1939–1994) was President of Associated (until 1990, Goshen) Mennonite Biblical Seminary for nearly twenty years and Professor of Systematic Theology. He is co-editor of *The Church's Peace Witness* (commended by Jürgen Moltmann). His collected essays are published in *The Theology of the Church* edited by Richard A. Kauffman and Gayle Gerber Koontz.

Jürgen Moltmann is Professor Emeritus of Systematic Theology in the Protestant Faculty of the University of Tübingen, Germany. Among his many publications are *Theology of Hope, The Coming of God, The Source of Life, God for a Secular Society, Experiences in Theology,* and *In the End—The Beginning.*

Willard M. Swartley is Professor Emeritus of New Testament at Associated Mennonite Biblical Seminary and the author of *Covenant of Peace: The Missing Piece in New Testament Theology and Ethics* and *Israel's Scripture Traditions and the Synoptic Gospels.* He is co-editor of *The Meaning of Peace* and editor of *Violence Renounced* and *Essays on Peace Theology and Witness.*

John Howard Yoder (1927–97) was President and Professor of Theology at Mennonite Biblical Seminary and then Professor of Theology at the University of Notre Dame. He is the author of *The Politics of Jesus, The Priestly Kingdom, To Hear the Word, When War Is Unjust,* and *He Came Preaching Peace.*

Perry Yoder is recently retired Professor of Old Testament at Associated Mennonite Biblical Seminary and the author of *From Word to Life* and *Shalom: The Bible's Word for Salvation, Justice, and Peace* and co-editor of *The Meaning of Peace.*

Editor's Foreword

This volume consists of two issues of *Occasional Papers*, No. 4 and No. 8, previously published by the Institute of Mennonite Studies (Elkhart, Indiana) during the time I served as Director of the Institute. Volume 4 (1983) carried the title of Professor Moltmann's Theological Lectureship, *Following Jesus Christ in the World Today*, presented both at the Associated Mennonite Biblical Seminaries (Elkhart, Indiana) and Canadian Mennonite Bible College (Winnipeg, Manitoba) in the fall of 1982. Volume 8, consisting of numerous responses from faculty at both institutions, was similarly titled, *Dialogue Sequel to Jürgen Moltmann's Following Jesus Christ in the World Today* (1984).

Both Moltmann's lectures and the faculty responses vigorously engage a range of theological issues arising from the moral dilemma that church *and* state raise for the shape of faithful discipleship. Moltmann's presentations, explicating and critiquing both Lutheran and Reformed (via Barth) resolutions of the moral dilemma, together with Anabaptist responses in the *Sequel*, define the shape of the issues under discussion. Some of the salient issues in this volume are noted by Miller and Harder in their co-authored introduction to Moltmann's lectures (see the Appendix). In the *Sequel*, Marlin Miller's "Introduction" and Thomas Finger's orienting essay, "Moltmann's Theology of the Cross," contribute helpful analyses and set a context for the dialogue responses. We are deeply grateful to Professor Moltmann for his willingness to read the responses and to respond critically and helpfully with his "A Response to the Responses." Perry Yoder's book review, concluding the *Sequel* and published by the *Conrad Grebel Review* (Winter, 1984), is included to make it a part of this larger forum of discussion. For Moltmann's additional essay to this publication, "Peacemaking and Dragonslaying in Christianity," I am also most grateful.

Emerging peace concerns within Europe in the early 1980s prompted in part Professor Moltmann's desire to become acquainted better with the Historic Peace Church tradition. Professor Moltmann's writings, especially *The Crucified God*, stimulated Mennonite interest in Moltmann's theology. The lectures here, published and edited anew, witness to the joining of these interests. The academic communities of the Associated Mennonite Biblical Seminaries and Canadian Mennonite Bible College were honored to be the hosts for Professor Jürgen Moltmann's visit to the United States in the fall of 1982, for the purpose of this dialogue and mutual benefit.

It was my task and pleasure to edit Moltmann's manuscript of the lectures. With his permission I also incorporated from the tapes some of his extemporaneous additions to and alterations of the written text. As noted in the original publication, I gratefully acknowledge the assistance of three people: Charmaine Jeschke for proofreading, Sue Yoder for typing the camera-ready copy, and Elaine Martin, IMS Administrative Assistant, for typing manuscript copy from parts of the tapes and managing the office work of the project. To prepare the text for this publication, I thank Rosalie Grove for scanning the essays, correcting errors, and noting points needing my attention.

I express my personal appreciation for Moltmann's contribution in these volumes, now joined into one. Whenever I read through this sequence of material (as I did several times earlier and now again) I do not do so without weeping as I conclude Moltmann's response. Amid the tears, I cry out, "Thy kingdom come; thy will be done on earth, as it is in heaven!"

—Willard M. Swartley
Professor Emeritus of New Testament
Associated Mennonite Biblical Seminary

Preface

It is good to be reminded of things, because we are not only reminded of what happened a long time ago, but also of hopes that were awakened in those experiences and which have been neither displaced nor forgotten. I am very grateful to my Mennonite friends in America for having reminded me of those years with this republication of the lectures I gave in Elkhart, Indiana, and Winnipeg, Manitoba, October 10–17, 1982.

It was 1981, at the highpoint of the Cold War between East and West, and the divided Germany was selected as the battleground. The Russians placed new SS20 atomic warheads in East Germany and the Americans answered with hundreds of Pershing 2 warheads and Cruise Missiles in West Germany. Nowhere else in the world was there such a military build-up as in the two parts of Germany. We sat literally on the powder keg of the Third and final World War. Our answer was a massive peace movement with human chains over three hundred kilometers long and the self-obligation of peaceful means. We sat in groups in front of the nuclear weapons arsenal full of courage and we protested—because we had to protest, not because we believed we would be successful. Ten years later the nuclear weapons were taken away, but we are still here.

The year 1981 actually became "The Year of the Sermon on the Mount" in West Germany. Not only bishops and theologians, but the Chancellor and even the President participated in public interpretation. The newspaper *Frankfurt Rundschau* printed the complete text of the

Sermon on the Mount on page two. Everyone felt how liberating on the one hand and how risky on the other was Jesus' proclamation in 1981. At that time in February 1981, as chair of the "Society for Protestant Theology" (Gesellschaft für Evangelische Theologie), I organized a large conference on the topic, "Discipleship and the Sermon on the Mount." We invited pastors and representatives of the historical peace churches, above all Mennonites; and we learned a great deal from their witness. We also discovered at that time the relevance of the Anabaptist movement during the Reformation era. We studied the Schleitheim Confession of 1527 and finally set up a gravestone for Michael Sattler and his wife at the gallows hill of Rotteneburg, where he was cruelly executed.

These are the reasons I gladly accepted the invitation in October of 1982 to the Mennonite conference in Elkhart, and afterwards in Winnipeg. I wanted to meet the Mennonites themselves and deliver my lectures in the Chapel of the Sermon on the Mount. I had never run across this name for a church before. We became very close at that time, as the dialog responses that are printed here demonstrate. The differences also became visible, but they are the differences among friends and co-workers for peace.

Some have asked: Where is the peace movement, which was so strong in our country in 1981? I want to say to them: In East Germany (DDR) there was also a peace movement of "Swords into Plowshares" which used the symbol of the USSR plowshare sculpture at the United Nations building in New York. The movement was suppressed, but a small circle gathered each Monday in the Nicholas Church (Nikolaikirche) in Leipzig to pray for peace. For eight years no one paid any attention to it. Then, however, a powerful demonstration wave emerged from this peace circle, and this church, with more than three hundred thousand people, who took a stand with candles and prayers for the reunification of Germany, called out: "We are the people." After six Monday demonstrations—which were carried out completely peacefully—the Berlin Wall fell. That was the first successful German revolution, and it was peaceful. Similar revolutions followed everywhere in Eastern Europe. Bismark had certainly contended that "one cannot govern a state with the Sermon on the Mount." And Lenin could only imagine a revolution by force. But there is an alternative, as history showed in 1989.

Today we stand before external and internal wreckage, which the unjust war in Iraq has left. This war was not an appropriate answer to September 11; but terrorism has only continued. There is another answer. We will have to look for it together, and I am certain that we can find it. I have therefore contributed a new article to this book on "Peacemaking and Dragonslaying in Christianity," which was originally published in 2004. I am pleased to make a new connection with Mennonite Christians with this book.

—Jürgen Moltmann
Tübingen, Germany
10 July 2005

Part I

Lectures by Jürgen Moltmann

1

The Lutheran Doctrine of the Two Kingdoms and Its Use Today

Introductory Statement

In its 400 years, established Protestantism on the Continent has developed two different theological conceptions in order to clarify, in its expression of Christian faith, its historical situation and its political commission. These two conceptions are the Lutheran doctrine of the two kingdoms and the Reformed doctrine of the lordship of Christ. These two doctrines define also the attitude which the German Protestant churches had toward the state during the church struggle under the Nazi dictatorship. On the basis of the two kingdoms doctrine, the Lutheran-established churches (the Landeskirche) maintained a "neutral" position as documented in the "Ansbach Decree" of 1935. On the basis of the doctrine of the lordship of Christ, which determines the whole of life, the Confessing Church took up the position of resistance, as shown by the "Barmen Theological Declaration" of 1934. Furthermore, the very strong differences in postwar Germany—to this day—over questions of politics and social ethics find their basis in the difference between these two conceptions.

Whether it has to do with questions of nuclear armament, the recognition of the Oder-Niss border, the contracts of the social-liberal government with the eastern Bloc, the ordering of private property, the question of abortion, the World Council of Churches' "Program to Combat Racism," or aid for development, division will appear along lines associated with these two doctrines again and again. On the one side—the side of the two kingdoms doctrine—these questions are defined as non-theological and are pushed away into the "kingdom of the world" to be dealt with only from the point of view of political reason and expedience; the other side, however, seeks to place political decisions within the meaning of obedient discipleship under the lordship of Christ.

The obstinacy with which both of these concepts are maintained shows that it is not simply two different models of theological ethics which are at stake here; rather, the roots of the difference lie in the understanding of the gospel, and of faith itself. In order for these models of theological ethics to be understood, it is necessary to clarify, therefore, the underlying understanding of the gospel contained within them. For without examination and clarification of the differing basic dogmatic positions there can be no change in the political orientation of the church and of faith. Only by rethinking these basic theological conceptions will new understandings emerge regarding the church's political commission in relation to the present day struggle for the liberation of the oppressed and for justice in the world. Some revision of these basic theological conceptions has been started by the recent political theology, and this promises to overcome some of the differences in the political orientations of the two conceptions. This political theology is ecumenical in character and is seeking, both in its Catholic and Protestant expressions, a new theological and ethical understanding of the church's commission in the political order.

The following lectures will introduce the most important aspects of these three theologies. They cannot, of course, be any more than an introduction, for each of these theologies is a world of its own, each having its own extensive library of exposition and polemic. In order to make a comparison possible, I will try to show how each of the three theological conceptions (designated by the first three lectures) stands in relation to three topics:

1. The basic theological position regarding Christology
2. The interpretation of eschatology and history
3. The relationship of theory and praxis

It is important to remember though that we are not dealing with Christian ethics for its own sake, but with the foundations of Christian theology and praxis.

The Two Kingdoms Doctrine

Although Lutherans constantly appeal to Luther's two kingdoms doctrine and its use in Lutheran tradition, there is no one uniform doctrine, but many. Even in Luther's writings and then also in the Lutheran tradition there are many very different doctrines of the two kingdoms. In Lutheran confessional documents (the so-called Book of Concord) there is no formulated two kingdoms doctrine. In the relevant Protestant dictionaries, two quite different articles on this doctrine often appear, both written by Lutherans. The Lutheran lawyer Johannes Heckel spoke of the "Garden of errors of the two kingdoms doctrine" and did not mean by that simply the immeasurable expanse of literature, but also the unclarity of the matter itself.

A look at actual practice increases the confusion: whereas some Lutherans in West Germany support politically conservative powers with the help of the two kingdom theory, Lutherans in East Germany live in and work with a socialist state by appealing to the same theory (see G. Jacob, *Weltwirklichkeit und Christus Glaube. Wider eine falsche Zwei-Reiche-Lehre,* 1977). While German Lutherans used this theory to justify favorable neutrality in the Third Reich, the Norwegian Bishop Berggrav used it to provide the rationale for his resistance against the Nazi tyranny. In the light of this "garden of errors," the two kingdoms doctrine does not appear to provide a particularly bright beam for guiding those pressed by political and ethical questions.

The Basic Theological Position: Apocalyptic Eschatology; History Is the Apocalyptic Conflict Between God and the Devil

Luther was an Augustinian monk. His early writings show him as an independent representative of the late medieval Augustinian renaissance. When he speaks of the two kingdoms in this early period he takes up Augustinian tradition and means by this the struggle of the *civitas Dei* (city of God) against the *civitas diaboli* (city of the devil), a conflict which rules world history until the end. The expressions *"civitas"* (city) and *"regnum"* (rule) can be interchanged, but it is always the conflict between *Jerusalem* and *Babylon,* between Cain and Abel, good and evil, God and the devil, which is meant when he speaks of the two kingdoms. The following diagram shows the two kingdom polarity.

FIGURE 1

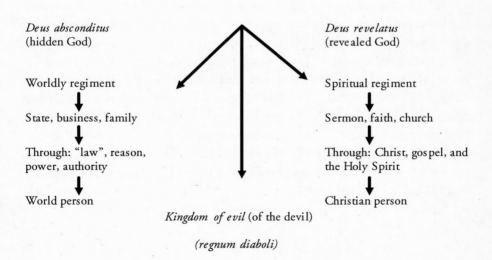

Kingdom of God

(regnum Dei)

Deus absconditus (hidden God)	*Deus revelatus* (revealed God)
Worldly regiment	Spiritual regiment
State, business, family	Sermon, faith, church
Through: "law", reason, power, authority	Through: Christ, gospel, and the Holy Spirit
World person	Christian person

Kingdom of evil (of the devil)

(regnum diaboli)

6

Just as this conflict between the two kingdoms dominates world history, it also dominates the personal life of the Christian as the *continual conflict of the Spirit against the flesh,* justice against sin, life against death, faith against unfaith. This struggle of faith which leads to the mortification of oneself and the vivification of the spirit will find its end only when the power of sin is conquered in the *resurrection of the body* and death is swallowed up in the victory of life. In principle, then, the battle between *God and the devil* in world history and in personal life is understood *eschatologically.* In fact, to be more precise, this eschatology is an apocalyptic eschatology which speaks of a real, but as yet, unrealized future.

But what is the cause of this conflict? In the Old Testament the cause of this struggle lies in the election of Israel to be the people of God in the midst of the godless nations, and in the election of the righteous who hold to the law of God in the midst of the lawless mass of human beings. Understood from a Christian perspective, the cause of the apocalyptic conflict of the end-time lies in the coming of Christ, the coming of the gospel and of faith. Through the *proclamation of the gospel* this conflict is inflamed, and through faith it is recognized (G. Ebeling). For the sake of the saving kingdom of Christ two kingdoms must be spoken of, for in salvation corruption is simultaneously revealed, and with the coming of Christ comes also the antichrist. The preaching of the gospel brings with the decision of faith the simultaneous separation of the faithful from the unfaithful, Christ from antichrist. This is not just an apocalyptic conflict which is going on. The cause of this conflict comes from God, in the election of Israel first and then in the coming of Christ and then in the coming of the gospel.

The decision of faith for God is always a decision against the devil. Thus this decision provokes an eschatological conflict in the world and in the life of every single person. Because God and faith go together, faith goes against the godless world; faith always contradicts this world and leads the person into temptation, trials, and suffering.

But, the two kingdoms theory which speaks of this conflict between the reign of God and the reign of evil (*diaboli*) would not be Christian if it were only to transmit this apocalyptic world view. Only when this conflict results from the coming of Christ and from the coming of faith, and Christ and faith are themselves the initiators of the eschatological conflict, does this two kingdoms theory have a Christian foundation. For the sake

7

of the kingdom of Christ, therefore, the *conflict* between the two kingdoms must be spoken of.

I will try to make this clear with the scheme in the above diagram. There are first the two kingdoms which are in the apocalyptic struggle: the kingdom of God and the kingdom of the devil. But inside of the kingdom of God, fighting against the evil and related also to the kingdom of the devil, there is the distinction between the worldly regiment and the spiritual regiment (or the worldly kingdom and the spiritual kingdom; the terms are not everywhere the same). So we have not only the doctrine of two kingdoms; we have the doctrine of four kingdoms. Sometimes Luther speaks of the two kingdoms with these two in mind; thus we must not confuse the church and the state, but recognize the difference and the cooperation of these two regiments *within* the struggle between the kingdom of God and the kingdom of the devil. (Parenthetically, though, can the devil have a kingdom? Or does the devil only give chaos, not a kingdom? But that's another question.)

When this distinction between the two regiments is clear, then two kingdoms within the reign of the world (*regnum mundi*) can also be spoken of. But what is "*the* world"? At this point the doctrine of the two kingdoms begins to become ambivalent; in the "Fall" the world raised itself in rebellion against God, but it is still God's creation. The devil has become "lord of this world," but God is still the creator of the world. As a result, the world finds itself in self-contradiction (Ebeling): it is godless, but God will not let it go. Because it has removed itself from its origin in God, destruction has fallen upon it. That it still remains, however, shows that God preserves it in spite of its turning away. Equally, every human being is also a creature and a sinner at the same time, and is both of them totally.

What also is the result of the kingdom of Christ in a self-contradictory world? The kingdom of Christ is set in contradiction against the kingdom of the devil, but it wants to save the world from this self-contradiction to make it again into God's good creation. The reign of Christ, therefore, is at one and the same time *against* the world as the kingdom of evil and *for* the world as God's creation, against human beings as sinners and for human beings as images of God. Further, two specific relationships between Christ's kingdom and the world appear in this theory: first, a relationship of contradiction is apparent when the kingdom of the world as the reign of evil or as the city of Babylon is opposed to the reign of Christ; second, a relationship of correspondence is apparent when the kingdom of the world, as creaturely, earthly and temporal, points toward the coming eternal kingdom of God. It is the same for the individual human being: the sinner is a contradiction to the Creator; but the one justified corresponds to the Creator. As long as history continues humans are constantly divided and in conflict within themselves.

It is, I believe, completely wrong to interpret the two kingdoms doctrine as either leaving the world as it is, or as dividing human beings into two parts, one which contradicts and opposes God, and the other part corresponding to God. That is not what the two kingdoms theory originally intended, although its adherents have often made just this of it. Authentically, this two kingdoms theory is far more concerned with two total aspects of the world and human beings—that is to say, two different perspectives: self-contradiction against God and correspondence to God. The total world and the whole person are meant every time. Contradiction and correspondence remain in conflict in every person's life and in the world itself until the end of the world.

The Dual Doctrine of the Two Kingdoms

Just as the two kingdoms doctrine has its theological origin in apocalyptic eschatology, it receives its ambivalence also from the same source: the kingdom of earth is, on the one hand, "this passing aeon of unrighteousness"; but, on the other hand, God is also Lord of this world in so far as he is Creator of it. The kingdom of the world is therefore also the kingdom of the earth (*regnum terrena*).

Within the basic distinction between the kingdom of God and the kingdom of evil which rules world history, the two kingdoms doctrine makes a second distinction between the saving kingdom of Christ and the life-sustaining kingdom of the world. Within this second distinction, both kingdoms—the kingdom of the world just as much as the kingdom of Christ—are directed against the kingdom of the devil but in different and therefore distinguishable ways.

Each of these kingdoms has its own justice: one has civil justice, the other the justice of God. In the kingdom of the world, law, good works, reason, the punishing sword and reward for good deeds are valid. In Christ's spiritual kingdom only grace, justification and faith are valid. In the worldly kingdom the sword rules; in the spiritual kingdom the word rules. In the spiritual kingdom God provides the eternal salvation. In the worldly kingdom people must take care of the temporal welfare.

Luther presented this distinction between the two kingdoms or regiments especially in his well-known pamphlet of 1523, "Of World Rulers, How Far One Is To Obey Them." My interest here is to clarify the fundamental perspectives of the two kingdoms doctrine through observing its use. Luther begins with the major distinction:

> Here we must divide Adam's children and all people into two parts: the first is those who belong to the kingdom of God, the rest belong to the kingdom of the world. Those who belong to the kingdom of God are all those who are true believers in and under Christ. For Christ is King and Lord in the Kingdom of God . . . and he also came that he might begin the kingdom of God and establish it in the world . . . The people need no worldly sword nor rights, and if all the world were true Christians, that is true believers, then there would be no prince, king, sword nor rights needed or used . . . To the kingdom of the world or under the law, however, belong all who are not Christian. For while few believe and the least conduct themselves according to the Christian manner, of not resisting evil and not doing evil, for those outside the Christian condition and the kingdom of God, God has created another regiment and has placed it under the sword . . . For if that were not so because, to be sure, all the world is evil and in every thousand there is scarcely one true Christian, each would devour the other. God has therefore ordained two regiments—the spiritual, made up of Christians and the pious people through the Holy Spirit under Christ; and the worldly regiment which restrains the non-Christians and wicked ones so that they must maintain outward order and be peaceful without their thanks (Clemen, 364ff.).

Luther distinguishes and demarcates each regiment then with respect to the other:

> If anyone attempted to rule the world by the gospel and to abolish all temporal law and sword on the plea that all are baptized and Christian

10

and that according to the gospel, there shall be among them no law or sword—or need for either—pray tell me friend, what would he be doing? He would be releasing the restraints and chains from the wild beasts and letting them bite and mangle everyone, meanwhile insisting that they are harmless, tame, and gentle creatures, but I would have the proof in my wounds. Just so would the wicked under the name of Christian abuse evangelical freedom, carry on their rascality, and insist that they were Christians subject neither to law nor sword, as some are already raving and ranting (Hertz, 63).

On the other side, Luther holds that

where the worldly regiment and law alone now rule, there must be futile hypocrisy, for it is as if they themselves are the same as the command of God. For without the Holy Spirit in their hearts no one will be truly pious, as many fine works as he may do. Where the spiritual regiment rules alone over land and people, however, there the restraints on viciousness will be untied and all wicked things will be given room (Clemen, 367).

According to Luther, both regiments mutually limit and complement the other. In the worldly regiment law and power serve to bring external order and earthly peace. In the spiritual regiment the word of God serves to bring to internal faith.

This distinction which Luther draws between the two is originally polemical; in the matter of faith there may be no laws nor coercion: "Faith is a free work to which no one can compel anyone." In the realm of faith, therefore, civil pressure and political oppression must not be used. Even heretics may only be overcome by means of the word of God and may not be politically persecuted. In the matter of faith it holds that "You must obey God more than humans." Wherever a ruler exercises political coercion in order to bring people to the faith of the country (Protestant or Catholic), he must be opposed. The ruler may not interfere with the kingdom of God nor with the spiritual regiment. On the other side, the spiritual regiment may not interfere with the worldly regiment, for one cannot rule the world with the Gospel.

Luther often also distinguishes between the two regiments anthropologically: the world regiment may not extend further than over the body, goods and the external parts of the earth. The spiritual regiment extends over the soul and the inner person. This description of the mutual limiting and complementing of the two regiments appears to be the description of an ideal state, but it was in fact critically directed by Luther as his contemporary religious and political situation. Why? Because, first, politics is constantly made to serve religion. This seduces and corrupts the soul. And second, religion is constantly made to serve politics. That corrupts worldly order and peace. Luther's two kingdoms doctrine was originally intended to enable Christians to make a critical-polemical separation between God and Caesar, to allow neither a Caesaro-papalism nor a clerical theocracy. It intended to teach that the world and politics may not be deified, nor may they be religiously administered. You should give to *Caesar* what belongs to Caesar—no more and no less—and give to *God* that which is God's. You should turn the self-deified world into the world, and let God be God. You should deal rationally with the world, with the law and with authority. The world is world and it will never become the kingdom of God; it is to be simply a good earthly order guarding against evil chaos. You should deal "spiritually" with God and his gospel—and here "spiritually" means faithfully. The gospel does not create a new world, but saves people through faith.

Christian Person and World Person

As illuminating as the great and small distinctions of the two kingdoms doctrine may be, when considered with regard to the Sermon on the Mount and the political life of the Christian, it has severe difficulties. Where are Christians to find a place to stand? On the law of the worldly regiment or on the gospel of the spiritual regiment?

First of all, Luther makes a corresponding distinction between faith which justifies before God without the works of the law and works which are to be done for the sake of the neighbor. When the person is justified before God by faith alone, then works will spring out of this justified relationship to God.

Liberated from the impossible task of earning access to heaven by way of works, these works now stand totally and exclusively in the service of the neighbor. In the distinction between faith and works we find again the distinctions which were operative in the two kingdoms theory. In faith, the human being is a Christian person; in works, a world person. This is again a critical-polemical distinction: whoever confuses faith and works will do justice to neither God nor the neighbor. Before God only faith helps; before the neighbor, only works help.

What is the standing of these good works for the neighbor? What criteria mandate and guide their expression? The Augsburg Confession says in Article XVI:

> The gospel teaches an eternal righteousness of the heart, but it does not destroy the state or the family. On the contrary, it especially requires their preservation as ordinances of God and the exercise of love in these ordinances.

The gospel does not create new orders in the world but calls instead for the preservation of the present orders, respecting them as "God's ordinances," and love is to be exercised within them. By ordinance here is meant the state, the economic system (socialism in the East and capitalism in the West) and the family. In these ordinances faith becomes effective through love.

The question, however, is: according to which guidelines should love be effective politically, economically and in the family? According to those of the law or of Christ? Indeed, at the end of Article XVI the Augsburg Confession says that one should obey the ruler and his laws in all these three areas of life, but then adds, "so that it may be done without sin."

Accordingly, Christian love in the worldly regiment stands under the law, by which is meant the law of God—the ten commandments and the natural law as well as the positive laws and decrees of the law books. The limitation upon such laws is that they should not force a person to sin, but this is mentioned without being more exactly formulated. It appears that God has set Christians within his two regiments, so that the Christian as Christ-person and world-person is a citizen of two kingdoms—the gospel and the law. In the spiritual regiment God rules through Christ and faith. In the worldly regiment God rules through the law without Christ.

This understanding has led Lutheran theologians to constantly conform to unjust forms of the state and business, because the criterion for justice in the kingdom of the world was missing. This view of the two kingdoms doctrine only arises, however, if one takes the distinction of both regiments out of the world-historical drama of the battle between the reign of God and the reign of evil, and deals with it in isolation on its own. The more both regiments are seen in their common struggle against the kingdom of evil, the closer they come together and so the clearer their common features become. As Melanchthon says in Article 198 of the Apology for the Augsburg Confession: "Through the good works of the faithful in the worldly regiment the kingdom of Christ reveals itself over against the power of the devil."

According to this view, Christian love in the various circumstances of political, economic and family life corresponds to the guideline of Christ. Through politics, business and family life, the Christian becomes God's co-worker and a witness to the kingdom of Christ against the kingdom of the devil. Christians will act appropriately and rationally in these various areas, but their deeds will be motivated by faith and will be directed toward the salvation of the world. The various areas of life give the place of Christian action but not the morality for these actions. The Christian acts in the relationships of the world but does not act under their compulsion.

Evaluation and Critique

I make several observations of Luther's two kingdom doctrine (see diagram above):

1. If we look from the spiritual to the worldly regiment we see the distinctions: here the Spirit, there the authority; here faith, there works; here gospel, there law.

2. If we look from the kingdom of God to the kingdom of the devil, then the spiritual and the worldly regiments come closer together: God fights the power of evil through both regiments—here with word and faith; there with order, peace and law.

14

3. If we only look at the differences between both regiments then the Christian stands in the contradiction of being a citizen of two different kingdoms: here required to be obedient to the gospel of the Sermon on the Mount and there required to be obedient to the law and authority of the state. But if we see that both regiments are together in God's battle against the devil, then the Christian, on the basis of faith in God, will do the good works of love against the devilish seed of hate in all worldly places. The worldly orders will thus become places in creation which all "contain Christ in themselves" (Wolf).

The eternal strife over the correct interpretation of Luther's two kingdoms doctrine has to do with these two perspectives and their ordering.

4. Insofar as Luther's two kingdom doctrine means the eschatological struggle between the reign of God and the reign of evil, it is a battle cry and its distinctions are polemical. But the main question is: *who* acts as judge in the two kingdoms theory? *Who* is allowed to draw the line of separation between the kingdom of the devil and the kingdom of God or between religion and politics? In East Germany we have a doctrine of the two kingdoms written out and lived out by the political party, the SAD. Marxists say, we take care of the body and you take care of the soul; we leave heaven to the theologians and take care of the earth. That is also a two kingdom theory. The political dictator of South Korea says we have freedom of religion but whoever draws political consequences out of his religion different from my policy will be put into jail. So there also is a two kingdom doctrine. Therefore it is very important to ask who makes the judgment as to where the line runs differentiating between the two lies. And *who* has the *right* to draw that line?

Misuses

Abusus non tollit usum, goes an old saying. However, when the misuse gains the upper hand, then it can be sensible to suspend a doctrine and to seek orientation in another place. I will mention, without systematic order, the misuses which have made the two kingdoms theory suspect for many Christians and theologians.

1. There was an inversion of this doctrine into its opposite when it was no longer employed critically-polemically for the sake of disentangling an entangled world, but was made instead into an ideology which affirmed the Protestant world. Instead of aiding the critical distinction to be made within both kingdoms, which are actually constantly mixed in history, it became a religious theory for two separate areas of the world: church and state. Instead of applying the dialectic of law and gospel, it became a dualism according to which the law of retribution and compulsion rules in the state and stood opposed to the rule of grace alone in the church. The more lawful and authoritative the state becomes, the purer and clearer the gospel of grace shines in the church. Bismarck was gladly celebrated as a divine hero of the worldly sphere. This separation of law and gospel in the 19th century, however, made the law graceless and the gospel lawless. Even today there are Lutherans who regret the repeal of the death penalty and with that the loss of the law of retribution. It was the socialists, like the German Minister of Justice, Gustav Radbruch, who translated the Sermon on the Mount into a legal order, according to which one should "pay back evil with good." They understood punishment in terms of education and re-socialization.

2. An inversion of the two kingdoms doctrine arose when, in the 19th century, the distinction between the spiritual and the worldly regiment was replaced by the distinction between private and public, or inner and outer. With that, faith was made world-less and the world was made faith-less. God became unreal and reality God-less. The world was left to unfaith, and faith retired into the shell of the introspection of the pious soul. It was believed that the two kingdoms doctrine was realized in the schizophrenia of the privatized, apolitical modern mind.

   The negative consequences of this misuse of the two kingdoms theory came to expression in Germany during the Hitler period.

16

The doctrine provided no basis for religious and political resistance to Hitler's perversion of the state and the political religion of national-socialism. For the most part, the church bowed with holy timidity before the autonomy of the political power struggle; it welcomed the fascist "law and order" and rejected the supposed chaos of democracy, liberalism and the Enlightenment. With this false separation of the two kingdoms, the gospel of the kingdom of Christ was made impotent on one hand and on the other, the right or arbitrariness was given over to the present powers.

Basic Theological Questions

1. The two kingdoms doctrine presents the gospel of Christ within an apocalyptic eschatology of the ongoing battle between the kingdom of God and the kingdom of the devil. This apocalyptic eschatology comes from the Old Testament; it was not developed from New Testament Christology. The two kingdoms doctrine paints Christology into the framework of this apocalyptic eschatology. Is that correct? Must not the gospel of Jesus Christ begin from the resurrection of Christ and God's victory over the power of evil in the cross? Apocalyptic eschatology understands Christ from within the world-historical struggle of God against evil, but it fails to understand history and the end of history from the viewpoint of Christ's victory. This is the questionable basic theological decision of the Lutheran two kingdoms theory; it begins with the struggle of faith with unfaith, and of God with Satan, but not from God's victory in Christ over sin, death and the devil. For the two kingdoms doctrine this victory lies in the apocalyptic future, but not in the prophetic and apostolic perfect tense. Therefore, the worldly orders are seen only as powers of repression against evil until the end, but not as processes open to the anticipating of the kingdom of God.

2. The two kingdoms theory places the worldly regiment under the law. It remains unclear, however, what the context of this law is: the covenant of Israel, natural law or the given laws which are

valid at the time of a certain society? Mostly, it is the latter, and with this consequence: these laws that are valid at the time within a certain society are also declared to be the laws of God—*tanquem ordinationes Dei* (as if they were the ordinances of God)! Lutherans therefore are called humorously the "eternal positivists." Where are the criteria for judging the justice of the valid laws in a given situation? Are there not *unjust laws*—legal laws which are laws that repress?

3. Finally, as this presentation shows, the two kingdoms theory gives no criteria for a specific Christian ethic. It gives criterion only for recognition of a secular ethic in a given society or an ethic of the worldly orders. Basically it is a theology of history but it is not a foundation for Christian ethics. It serves to sharpen the conscience; that is its strength. It brings into Christian ethics a realism which reckons with the given facts. But it does not motivate world-transforming hope. That is its weakness.

Sources: The quotations from Luther are Moltmann's translation of Otto Clemen, *Luthers Werken in Auswahl,* vol. 2 (Berlin: de Gruyter, 1929); one is from the English work edited by Karl H. Hertz, editor, *Two Kingdoms and One World: A Sourcebook in Christian Social Ethics* (Minneapolis: Augsburg, 1976).

2

Barth's Doctrine of the Lordship of Christ and the Experience of the Confessing Church

The recently formulated doctrine of the *lordship of Christ* provides an alternative to the doctrine of the *two kingdoms*. The doctrine of the lordship of Christ has developed out of the Reformed tradition, called by some the Calvinistic or theocratic tradition.

The impulse toward the present doctrine of the lordship of Christ has come from the theology of Karl Barth and the *Confessing* German Church under the German dictatorship of Hitler. Its basic formulation is to be found in the "Barmen Theological Declaration" of 1934, Theses 1 and 2:

> **Thesis 1:** Jesus Christ, as he is witnessed to us in Holy Scripture, is the one Word of God which we have to hear, to trust in life and death, and to obey.
>
> We reject the false teaching that the church can and must also recognize still other events, powers, forms and truths as the revelation of God, outside and alongside this one Word of God.

Thesis 2: As Jesus Christ is God's consolation for the forgiveness of all our sins, so and with equal seriousness is he also God's powerful demand over our entire life; through him a joyous liberation from the godless bondage of this world comes to us for the free, thankful service of all his creatures.

We reject the false teaching that there can be areas of our life in which we have lords other than Jesus Christ, areas in which we do not require justification and sanctification from him.

A short exposition of these theses of the Confessing Church should serve to highlight the thinking underlying them.

All the confessions of the Reformation are essentially christocentric: the Church enters into its truth when Christ—and indeed Christ alone—is its Lord. The church enters its freedom when it listens to the gospel of Christ, and indeed only to that gospel and to no other voice. Therefore all human church laws and all church statues are placed under the measure of the gospel of Christ.

The Confessing Church repeated this central confession in the face of the totalitarian claims of the state, the nation and the society. Whenever political powers and social interests want to make the church into their servant, the lordship of Christ—and indeed, the exclusive lordship of Christ over his church—must be confessed and witnessed to in the form of resistance. Only under the lordship of Christ is the church free; only so can it be a liberating people. It can never become a vassal of other powers and an accomplice of organized injustice without losing its identity.

There are no places in the world that are excepted and in which the liberating lordship of Christ is ineffective. The experience of liberation from the godless bondage "of this world" shows itself in the free and thankful service of all God's creatures. Therefore, the liberating power of Christ penetrates, redeems and claims the whole of life, including its political and economic relationships. Those who would restrict the lordship of Christ to a spiritual, churchly or private area, thus declaring other areas of life to be autonomous, fundamentally deny the lordship of Christ.

With these theses of the Barmen Declaration, the Confessing Church freed the public form of the Church from the claims of state ideology and political religion: "the church must remain the church." With the first thesis the German-Christian heresy was rejected. It claimed: "Christ for the soul; Hitler for the people." Or, "the Gospel for faith; the law of the German nation for ethics." In this area of church opposition to Hitler and his fascist regime, the Confessing Church had success.

But as soon as the question of political resistance to Hitler became acute the Confessing Church entered into difficulty. The second Barmen thesis led to conflicts of conscience, when the war began. When drafted, confessing Christians also marched into war for Hitler, although "in faith" they rejected him and the war as an unjust war. Political opposition to Hitler was exceptional; Dietrich Bonhoeffer, for example, was an exception when discipleship of Christ drove him into politics and into conspiracy against Hitler. It is still an unresolved discussion in German theology whether inner-church resistance is sufficient or whether this must be extended to political resistance. Should Christians react only when the state intrudes into the church and, for example, dismisses or imprisons Jewish-Christian clergy or socialist priests? Or must they react as soon as socialists themselves are persecuted, Jews are murdered and whole races or classes are oppressed? Must we resist only when the church and witness to faith is suppressed or should we resist whenever injustice appears as a public issue. How wide does the liberating—and therefore, commanding—Lordship of Christ extend? How can Christians respond to their Lord in the political struggles of the present? Before we deal with these current questions, we must first clarify, for ourselves, the basic theological position which lies behind the doctrine of the all-embracing lordship of Christ.

The Basic Theological Position: Christological Eschatology

The Barmen Theological Declaration begins with the assumption that God in Christ has fully and finally revealed himself and that, therefore, there are no other sources of divine revelation for the church. God reveals himself in his Word, Jesus Christ. He does not, therefore, also reveal himself in history, in nature, in political movements or political leaders. These stand rather in contrast to Christ, in opposition to his revelation. God has not revealed himself ambiguously; he has revealed himself unambiguously.

The second thesis of the Barmen Declaration concludes from this that Jesus Christ is already, here and now, the Lord of all the universe, of the powers and, so, of the whole of human life. Therefore there are no areas, in which the Christian must also listen to other voices, powers, or laws alongside the voice of Christ. All things and all relationships now stand under the liberating and claiming lordship of Christ. This is already accomplished.

This basic theological position is expressed clearly in the theology of Karl Barth. In three topical publications from the years of the church struggle, Barth attempted to grasp and define the relationship of church and world christologically. These were: *Gospel and Law* (1935); *Justification and Justice* (1938); *The Christian Community and Civil Community* (1946). These three titles already show the direction of his thought: from Christ to church, from church to politics, from faith to life and from religion to the kingdom of God. The basic idea is this: in Christ God has humbled himself and has taken on the whole of humanity. God has lowered himself even to death on the cross and has taken on the whole misery of human life, namely its rejection. In Christ, God has exalted the human being and has brought the human being to freedom and honor. Therefore Christ is the reconciler who takes away sin and condemnation from human persons. Because Christ does this, he is also the victor over all powers and authorities. His resurrection from the dead and his exaltation to lordship reveal the triumph of God's grace. Death is already swallowed up in his victory. The exalted Lord already ushers all powers and authorities behind himself in triumphal procession.

From this basic christological position three controversial consequences arise for Barth:

1. The whole world is already objectively in Christ and is placed under his lordship. No longer is there a world-historical struggle between God and the devil. The struggle has already been decided in Christ. The victory has been revealed in Christ's resurrection. Christian faith lives in the certainty of Christ's victory over sin, death and the devil. The decision about this world has already been made by God for the sake of its salvation. Objectively, i.e., from God's point of view, in Christ all humans are already reconciled. Subjectively, however, i.e., seen from a human point of view, there are both the faithful, who recognize their reconciled being, and the unfaithful, who do not recognize it: "Knowledge

22

of God is one thing, being in God is another" ("The Christian Community," 5). Barth has replaced Luther's apocalyptic eschatology with a christological eschatology. Out of the constant battle between God and evil, God's victory over the devil has come in Christ. This victory has been already obtained in Christ for all people, once for all. The eschatological future remains, therefore, only as the public and universal unveiling of this victory of Christ.

2. If Christ is Lord, then already all power in heaven and on earth is given to him. It also follows that "the state as such belongs originally and finally to Jesus Christ; its relatively independent substance, its dignity, function and objective are to serve the person and work of Jesus Christ" ("Justification").

    For a long time Barth tried to ground this thesis in a strange exegesis of Romans 13. Günther Dehn believed that the *exousiai-*powers which are named there are angelic powers. As all angels serve already the exalted Lord, so also are the political powers subject to Christ. If that were so, then the consequence would be a christological metaphysic of the state. Later Barth gave up this exegetical interpretation. The thesis of the New Testament is not that of a Christian metaphysic of the state but is rather that of a Christian ethics in politics. It is not a theological doctrine of the state which is taught, but rather a theological substantiation for Christian discipleship, i.e., how Christians should behave in the political area. In contrast to the Lutheran tradition which isolated Romans 13 from its context and thus used the text to formulate a Christian view of the state, Romans 13 must be seen in the context of Romans 12 which addresses how Christians should respond to evil and, then in chapter 13, specifically to government. Romans 13, therefore, should not be used as a theological umbrella to cover or justify the acts of the state.

3. Above all, Barth saw that the New Testament describes the order of the new creation with political and not with religious concepts: the kingdom of God (*basileia*), heavenly city (*polis*), heavenly citizenship (*politeuma*). Barth draws the conclusion that "The real earthly church sees its future and hope not in a heavenly reflection

of its own existence but precisely in the real heavenly *state*" ("Justification"). Its promise and hope is not the eternal triumphal church but the state built by God coming from heaven to earth ("Christian Community"). Thus the incomplete earthly state and the incomplete human society are oriented toward the coming lordship of God.

Thus in this basic theological position of Barth we find:

a. "Christological eschatology" in which "Jesus is victor." Christian faith lives everywhere in the certainty of Christ's victory.

b. Universal Christology in which Christ is the Pantokrator: "For through him was everything created that is in heaven and on earth, seen and unseen" (Col 1:16). From this perspective the world-historical struggles are only the rear-guard actions of an already defeated enemy.

c. The christological ethic of obedient discipleship in all areas of life, i.e., an ethic of the relationship of created life to the reconciling God! The question to be put here, however, is: according to which measure and in which direction must the discipleship of Christ take place?

The Christian Community and the Civil Community

With all possible emphasis, Barth distinguishes between church and state—which, however, are bound together in a unity of basis and aim—in that he speaks of two different communities, rather than two kingdoms.

The church is the Christian community. It is the community of those people in a particular place who as *Christians* are called out from the rest into the elect through the knowledge and confession of Jesus Christ. The church is concrete in the "gathering of the faithful" (*Ecclesia*). Its life is defined inwardly through the one faith, one love and one hope, and outwardly through common confession and common proclamation of the gospel to all people.

The civil community is the community of all people in one particular place who are bound together through a common legal order. The purpose of their community is the securing of the outer, relative freedom of each person and the outer relative peace of their community. In so far as this happens, the civil community provides the provisional and preliminary form for corporate human life. That Barth characterized the civil community as a *legal community,* and not as a *ruler* with a monopoly of authority, is important. Law and the establishing of justice, therefore, is the foundation of this state, even when adherence to the law is enforced by means of force.

In the civil community both Christians and non-Christians are together; they are limited regionally, that is to say, nationally. In the Christian community only the faithful are together, and they are together in ecumenical freedom and expanse. The Christian community is held together by the consciousness of God; in the civil community, however, the relationship to God cannot be an element of the legal order. The Christian community recognizes the necessity of belonging, in its own being, to various civil communities. It recognizes the legal order and the necessity of its protection by means of force. In this legal order, the Christian community sees a divine ordering, a constancy of divine providence over against human sin; this ordering is an instrument of divine grace, a point similarly advanced in the two kingdoms theory.

But how should the Christian community act in and upon the civil community? Barth always remained firmly against the dissolution of Christianity into a political movement of either the right or of the left: "the church must remain the church." Precisely because the church is the church of Jesus Christ which concentrates entirely upon its Lord, it affects the civil community.

Barth's thought on the relationship of the Christian and civil communities may be presented in a diagram consisting of concentric circles around Jesus Christ as the center, as follows:

FIGURE 2

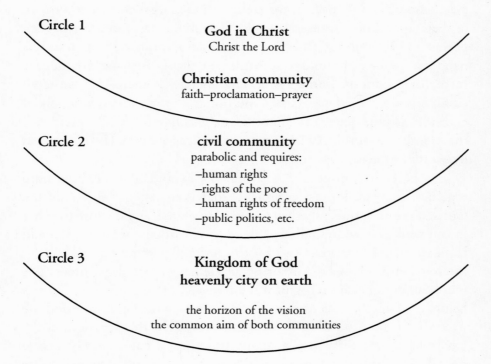

Circle 1

God in Christ
Christ the Lord

Christian community
faith–proclamation–prayer

Circle 2

civil community
parabolic and requires:
  –human rights
  –rights of the poor
  –human rights of freedom
  –public politics, etc.

Circle 3

Kingdom of God
heavenly city on earth

the horizon of the vision
the common aim of both communities

The Christian congregation is the inner circle of the kingdom of Christ. It proclaims the liberating lordship of Christ and the hope of the coming kingdom of God. The civil community, even in the best of possible circumstances, does not do that. Precisely in the fulfilling of its own task the Christian community also joins with the task of the civil community but, as it were, in an indirect way. Because the church has faith in Jesus Christ and proclaims him, it believes and proclaims him who, as the head of his church, is the lord of the world. In this proclamation it confronts all political concepts with its hope, and also with its critique. This faith and proclamation is valid then especially for *political realities,* and in this twofold way.

First, the church's proclamation will destroy human hubris, pride and arrogance, which is present in all political ideologies and lordships; and it will point sharply to their eschatologically provisional character. But it will also resist resignation and compromise which characterizes political actions; in this way it extends the hope of the eschatological completion of politics into the city of God. At the same time, the church will not erect a Christian doctrine of the state nor religiously justify and bless the political condition. Because the Christian community concentrates itself upon the proclamation of Christ as the Lord, it holds the political processes accountable, keeping them open for the kingdom of God. Politics remains earthly—a forever provisional process for freedom and justice. This condition is difficult to bear. But whoever wants to claim finality for or reify this political process will become a tyrant. Also, whoever yields this process to resignation delivers the world over to the tyrants. The direct effect of the proclamation of Christ and the Christian community upon the civil community is that political conditions are kept changeable and the political changes are kept historically incomplete. The church does not divinize politics nor does it demonize politics. It places politics into the human sphere, thus "suspending" it for permanent improvement and historical incompleteness. That is the first step.

Second, out of this condition of suspension which has been brought about by the Christian community's proclamation and existence, there follows for Barth a subsequent step, which is best initially formulated as a question: "Are there directions and guidelines for Christian decisions which are to be executed within the political sphere? The state is not and never will become the kingdom of God; nevertheless it stands under the promise of the coming kingdom of God. How is this to be comprehended? Barth uses the language of *parable* in dealing with this condition of suspension. There is no exact similarity between the state and the kingdom of God, but there is also no absolute dissimilarity. Their relationship is to be perceived as that of *parable,* correspondence, and analogy; this approach understands the justice of the state from the Christian view of the kingdom of God, believed in and proclaimed by the church.

Politics, like culture, is thus capable of acting as a parable, a picture of correspondence, for the kingdom of God, and necessarily so. Because of this, Barth calls the civil community the outer circle of the kingdom of Christ. Since the Christian community as inner circle and the civil community as outer circle have their common center in Christ the Lord and their common aim in the kingdom of God, the Christian community, by means of its *political* decisions, will urge the civil community to act as a parable by corresponding to God's justice and not contradicting it. It wants the state to point toward, and not away from, the kingdom of God.

The church wants the grace of God to be represented in the outer, provisional deeds of the political community. But how is this to happen? Barth gives some examples:

a. The Christian community lives from the God who has become human. Therefore, for the church, the state and the law exist and function for the sake of human life; humans do not exist for the sake of the state and the law. Since God has become human, the human becomes the measure of all things political. Therefore Barth turns against Moloch "nationalism" and against humanly destructive "capitalism."

b. The Christian congregation is the witness to the divine justification of human beings. Its maxim, therefore, is: justice precedes power;" it must then step in against anarchy and tyranny.

c. The Christian community is the witness to the Son of Man who came to seek those who are lost. It will therefore take the side of the lost, the weak, the poor and those threatened. It will choose from the differing socialist possibilities the one from which it expects the greatest social justice.

d. The Christian community is called into the freedom of the children of God. It will involve itself politically, therefore, for the sake of human and civil rights. "It will not under any circumstance support a practical dictatorship, or partial and temporary restrictions of civil freedoms; it will certainly oppose, under all circumstances, the principle of dictatorship.

e. The Christian community lives from the light of the public revelation of God in Christ. The necessary political analogy to this consists in the existence of the Christian community as the resolute opponent of all secret politics and secret diplomacy. Where freedom and responsibility in the service of the civil community are one, everything can and must be spoken before all ears and dealt with before all eyes.

Barth consciously restricted his discussion in this essay ("Community") to examples of Christian political positions in order to make clear his basic thought: politics has parabolic capacity and is equally necessary, therefore, to the lordship of Christ in both the beliefs of the Christian community and the community's public proclamation.

This requires, however, that "the right and proper state must have its image and example in the right and proper church. So the church exists in an exemplary way; i.e., so that, through its simple presence and its way of being present, it is the source of renewal and the power of preservation for the state."

The proclamation of the lordship of Christ would amount to nothing if the church did not begin first, in its own life, its constitution, its government and its administration, to witness practically to this lordship of Christ.

Summary, Evaluation, and Critique

1. The Christian community and the civil community have different commissions in history, but they have their common foundation in Christ the Lord and their common aim in the kingdom of God. Therefore not only their differences may be established, but because of their common foundation and their common orientation, correspondences, parables and analogies must be sought.
2. The state is not seen as a repressive authority of God against evil but as an outer, earthly and provisional vessel for the good. It is not understood as a repressing power against chaos and sin, as is so clear in the description of the state in Luther. Understood as the civil community and as the community of law, the state contains the positive possibilities of a parable of the kingdom of God.
3. Whereas, according to Lutheran doctrine the Christian is required to act in the worldly regiment only according to the principles of reason, choosing the means for the ends and limiting love for the neighbor to political ends, Barth's parable theory gives substantial criteria and guidelines for Christian political action. Christian faith does not only free political reason *to be itself with its own rationality,* as the Lutherans say, but also, according to Barth, uses political

29

reason, by virtue of its interest in making claims upon people, to make visible in parable-form the kingdom of God here on earth.

Barth's political parable theory is often ridiculed because of his illustration of the Christian necessity for rejecting secret services and secret diplomacy: "That this argument is theologically and politically indefensible is immediately clear," says Helmut Thieliche. Or it is said that the impression given is that these examples were selected at random, that the analogies are only developed in an exemplary and playful way. Or Barth is criticized for having underestimated the problem of the "relative autonomy" and self-responsibility of the political arena.

But when we read his essay more carefully and ask ourselves which political conception lies behind it, one discovers the basic elements of social democracy as the precursor and the best available correspondence to the lordship of Christ and the kingdom of God. It is in this context that Barth calls for the public transparency of all political decisions. It fits into the fundamentally *democratic* claim of socialism, which theologically and politically is immediately obvious and is in no way to be ridiculed.

4. For Barth, democratic socialism was not the kingdom of God on earth. It would also never become that. But for Barth it was the best possible parable of the kingdom of God which is readily present and therefore provisional. Thus Barth's political option of democratic socialism was never simply and affirmatively expressed as "Christians for socialism" but was always simultaneously critical: "Socialism for the sake of the kingdom of God." That means exactly as far as it corresponds to the kingdom of God and does not contradict it.

Misuses

The above diagram makes the picture so simple that it is hardly protected against misuse. Barth's ordering of the church as prior to state and society can easily lead to a clerical tutelage whether that be from the theological left or right. His demand that the Christian community be "an example" for the civil community can only be fulfilled by that church which Barth calls "the true church." But where is "the true church?" The actual church with its feudal constitution, its anachronistic symbols and rites and its outdated languages is in most cases less like the forerunner of the civil community than it is the tail-light of cultural development. If the possibility and the power to create parables for the lordship of Christ in political life depend upon the precedence and example of the Christian community, then Barth's theory fails in the practice.

How, for example, can the Roman Catholic church be against secret politics and demand public access to political dealing and processes, when its own Sacred Congregation of the Faith does not hold even to the fundamental principles of present legal practice, and does not even inform the accused of the charges (as, e.g., in the case of Hans Küng)? How can a German Protestant church be on the side of democracy in public life when it rejects the democratization of its own constitution and does not proceed from the rights of the (Christian) person? Barth knew the condition of the churches. He complains about them at the end of this pamphlet. He should have begun with this criticism, in order not to become theologically illusionary.

Two Critical Theological Questions of the Basic Foundation

1. The doctrine of the lordship of Christ over the Christian community and the civil community is grounded in *Christological eschatology:* Christ is the Pantokrator who already now rules over heaven and earth. This Christology is present initially and powerfully in the early Christian hymns and then in the letters to the Ephesians and Colossians. These hymns actually proclaim the present lordship of Christ already broken out over the world and the complete subjection of the cosmic and political power already taken place. Christians already participate in the complete lordship of Christ in doxological jubilation. They are already raised with Christ. They participate in his resurrected Lordship. They already RULE WITH HIM! But that is, according to Ernst Käsemann, an enthusiastic piety which forgets the crucified one and retreats from the reality of the world.

Paul certainly opposed this so-called "Corinthian enthusiasm" and he taught over and over again that the lordship of Christ is none other than the rule of the crucified one. In the present, Christians have an immediate part in the cross, but they do not already have any immediate part in the resurrection glory of Christ. The certainty of the victory of faith is a certainty only under the cross and nowhere else. Indeed Barth seldom speaks of a "kingly" lordship of Christ. He restricts himself to the language of the "lordship of Christ." It must be stressed against his students and also against him too that the lordship of Christ is not like that of a king's but is the lordship of the crucified who does not conquer with great might but through his weakness, and who rules by his representative suffering on the cross. Christ's lordship is the lordship of the slain Lamb!

Without the living memory of the death and cross of Christ, the doctrine of the kingly rule of the lordship of Christ will become triumphalist and theocratic. It becomes self-justifying. But Christ is no super-king—the King of Kings—and he is also no Superstar, but he is the Son of man whose "power is made perfect in weakness" (RSV, 2 Cor 12:9). It probably belongs together with the memory of the crucified one that Paul does not confer the risen one with the title of Cosmocrator nor with the statement that all the kingdoms and the powers of this world have been already subjected to Christ. According to 2 Corinthians 15:28 God will make everything subject to his Christ *in the future;* then the Son will hand the kingdom over to his Father. That Christ is the Lord signifies for Paul that he *must* rule "until all his enemies lie under his feet." Only then, when the lordship of the crucified becomes God's, will the lordship of all earthly lords, rulers and authorities, along with death, be destroyed.

Thus what for Barth is already completed in the cross and resurrection of Christ has not yet happened for Paul. What is certain victory for Barth is the certainty of hope for Paul.

2. Barth's doctrine of the already present lordship of Christ over all lords, rulers and powers, leads to the following ambiguity: either all powers and states serve the Pantokrator Christ already, whether

they know it or not, or the Pantokrator rules over the Christians and only through them can he rule in all civil areas of this world. Then his rule reaches as wide as the obedience of the faithful.

In *Justification and Justice* Barth says that "the proclamation of justification as the proclamation of the kingdom of God establishes true justice and the true state here and now" (p. 25). That leads to a Christian metaphysic of the state. Against this, in the "Christian Community and Civil Community" Barth says, "The Christian community is not in a position to propose a doctrine such as the Christian doctrine of the just state"! (p. 12–13). If, on the basis of the world-rule of Christ, a Christian doctrine of the state was produced, it would then be difficult, with 1 Corinthians 15:26, to expect the destruction of all rulers, principalities and powers. The post-Barthian discussion in Germany has therefore distanced itself totally from a theological theory of the state. The lordship of Christ, according to our experience, reaches as far as people who, freed from sin through Jesus' death, are obedient. There are certainly directions given for the discipleship of Christians in political life which arise from Jesus' lordship, but there is no metaphysic of the state which is equally valid for Christians and non-Christians. Christocentric ethics can only be discipleship ethics. It is an ethic for Christians in a state, but not a Christian ethic for the state. It is political ethics for the Christian community but not Christian politics for the civil community.

Sources: For text and commentary on the Barmen Confession see Ernst Wolf, *Barmen; Kirche zwischen Versuchung und Gnade* (Munich: Chr. Kaiser, 1975) and Arthur C. Cochrane, *The Church's Confession Under Hitler* (Philadelphia: Westminster, 1962).

3

Political Theology and Political Hermeneutics

The Lutheran *two kingdoms* doctrine arose out of the Reformation. The Reformation happened 400 years ago in the power of the newly discovered gospel and was related to the medieval *corpus Christianum*—"Christendom." It had immediate consequences for the relationship of church and secular institutions to one another and for the life of Christians in both.

The new *lordship of Christ* doctrine arose out of the resistance of the Confessing Church. This resistance lived out of the power of the gospel and was related to the modern secularized state and the anti-Christian, totalitarian ideology of the state. In post-war Germany the effect of the Confessing Church was repressed by the restoration of the old church-state relationships. In place of a "free church" in a "free state" there arose a new institutionalized partnership between the established churches and the state which was secured through church contracts (on the Protestant side) and Concordats (on the Roman Catholic side). The romantic idea of the "Christian West" versus the Communist East encompassed the churches, the state, the schools and the society. This "utopia of the status quo" was attractive in the Federal Republic of Germany from 1945 until the beginning of the 60's, because, understandably so, many people after their experience of the chaos of war sought only order and security.

What Is Political Theology? What Does It Want?

The new concept of a *political theology* has arisen out of a deep dissatisfaction with this restoration of antiquated conditions in Germany. In contrast to Barth, it began with criticism and a new definition of the social and political functions of the church under the conditions of the modern age. In Germany, this concept was the first attempt at a critical society-related theology in which Catholic and Protestant theologians participate in the same way (e.g., Johan Baptist Metz on the Catholic side and Dorothee Sölle and myself on the Protestant side). Political theology also has a cross-confessional character and is ecumenical insofar as both churches stand before the same problem of the growing irrelevance of their doctrines and ethics for modern life, finding in none of the different theological-church traditions the *key* for the solution of the problems of the modern age.

This new political theology for the church and Christian life under the conditions of the European modern age has two starting points.

First, the process of secularization has not yet received a sufficient theological answer or explanation. Political theology has taken up the Marxist criticism of religion in this process. This is, as is well known, not a criticism of the content of Christian theology and religious faith but only a functional criticism, a criticism of the social, political and psychological functions of religion and church. It is no longer asked whether a theological doctrine is true or false; instead, it is tested practically to see whether its effects are oppressive or liberating, alienating or humanizing. With this, *praxis* becomes the criterion of truth. This is true not only for Marx, but it is operative from Kant to Sartre; it is the characteristic feature of the modern spirit. It is a movement from *orthodoxy* to *orthopraxy*. With this criterion, reflective consciousness has no longer a self-forgetting contemplative relationship to reality but has won an immanent, operative and therefore self-critical relationship to reality instead.

A theology which engages in this must reflect constantly and critically, therefore, upon its practical functions, as well as upon its content. A church which engages in this may no longer ask abstractly about the relationship of "the church and politics," as if these were two separate things which must be brought together; rather, this church must begin with a critical awareness of its own political existence and its actual social functions.

Political theology is not a new dogmatic, but it wants to awaken the political consciousness of every Christian theology; it wants to be a *fundamental* theology, as J. B. Metz says. There is theology which is conscious of its own political function; there is also naive and, politically unconscious theology. But there is no *a*political theology; neither in earth nor in heaven (since we expect a heavenly *politeuma*). There are churches who do not want to recognize their political "Sitz im Leben" within their society. They conceal, cover and disguise it and then assert that they are politically "neutral"—something which they *de facto* never are. There are Christian groups who exist consciously as Christian groups. But there is never an *a*political church—neither in history nor in the kingdom of God. "Political theology" does not want to make political, rather than theological, questions the central concern of theology, but rather the reverse: it wants to be thoroughly Christian, especially in its public and political functions. It doesn't want to "politicize" the church but it does want to "Christianize" the political involvement of Christians. It therefore takes up the modern functional criticism of religion and urges movement from the orthodoxy of faith to the orthopraxis of discipleship of Christ.

Second, the history of the modern age will not be understood if it is seen theologically as only negative, i.e., the modern emancipation from tradition, the secularization of the holy, or the defection of the world from God and the church. Modern consciousness criticizes the past and the traditions regarding the origins and meaning of the past because it is oriented towards the future; it organizes human life for the end and fulfillment of history.

The criticism of past reality takes place in the name of present possibilities for the future. The criticism of tradition and institutions seeks freedom for the new present and the hoped-for-future. Thus Kant was the first to put the modern question to religion: "What may I hope for?" Instead of dwelling upon metaphysical origins as a source for security, humanity looks now to the future for transcendent meaning, an important and perhaps unique development in Western Christian theology. The experience of transcendence is thus shifted out of metaphysics into eschatology.

Following the primacy of love in medieval theology and the primacy of faith in the reformation theology, the modern age disclosed the primacy of hope. Immanence is no longer experienced as the transient earth under an immortal heaven, but as an open process of life and as the history of a still unknown future. For 150 years theology and church had not understood this modern primacy of the future and the modern struggle for the truth of hope. Because both theology and the church encountered this development in forms of criticism of the church and of social revolution, they felt forced into a defensive position and allied themselves with anti-revolutionary powers and conservative ideologies. They saw the future of the modern age simply as the image of the antichrist and its hope as the spirit of blasphemy. Only recently have we learned to understand that the modern situation calls us to "account for the hope that is in us" (1 Pet 3:15). This "account" is no longer achieved theologically with a small tractate on "the moral perfections," as was the case traditionally where hope was only briefly dealt with together with the other virtues of faith and love. Rather, this "account" requires a new eschatological orientation of the whole of Christian theology in order that theology can respond with the biblical promissory history to the modern interest in the history of the future.

The new political theology therefore, has declared eschatology as its foundation and as the medium of Christian theology, and this stands in contrast to the expectation of merely an apocalyptic moment in the future, as conceived in the older theology. It has designed Christian theology into a messianic theology. The roots of political theology in Europe lie in "the theology of hope."

The Basic Theological Position: Eschatological Christology

When one speaks of Christology, it sounds specifically *Christian,* but it is really not so. The doctrine of the Christ is the doctrine of the anointed messiah, the hoped-for-liberator and the awaited redeemer. There is also

Jewish and Islamic messianism and messiology. There is messiology in every doctrine of salvation and every liberation ideology.

The modern age also has developed its political messianisms: National socialism declared the nation to be the Messiah; Italian fascism spoke of the "Duce" of the end-time; German national socialism worshipped the "Führer" of a "Third" or thousand-year Reich; Saint Simon named "the machine" as messiah because it would liberate us from toil and work; and in early Marxism, the proletariat who freed themselves became the "redeemed redeemer" of the world. Everywhere in the modern age the primacy of the future was recognized and people themselves organized the end of history. Political and social revolutionary messianism arose as a result.

With political theology, however, we come to a very specific messianism, the messianic theology of the historical Jesus and the Jesus of the cross. The distinctive features of this messianic Christology do not lie in its orientation toward the future, nor simply in a present liberation from misery, but in the definition of the *subject* of this Christology: who is the Christ? Who is the Messiah? Christian Christology believes that the Christ is not a nation nor a Führer nor a People nor a Spirit but, *Jesus of Nazareth*—the one sent with the gospel of the kingdom to the poor, the preacher of the Sermon on the Mount, the one who called his followers to discipleship, and the one who was crucified under Pontius Pilate, was raised from the dead by God, and will come to judge the living and the dead. Not Christology or messianism as such, but *Jesus* makes the messianism of the political theology we here describe as specifically *Christian.*

If Christian theology, therefore, really wants to understand Jesus as the *true Christ,* then it must grasp him and his history in an eschatological way. It must read the story of Jesus within the framework of the Old Testament history of promise in order to understand his conflict with the law and his fulfillment of the Old Testament promise. It must so interpret his death and his resurrection from the dead in the light of the Old Testament hope in the coming God in order to understand him as the liberator of the world sent from God. Jesus is understood historically only if his story is read in light of the remembered hope of the Old Testament and the awakened hope of the kingdom of God. In this way then he is understood as God's Christ.

This brings us then to the very old Christ-question, put by the Jewish people: "Are you the coming one or shall we wait for another?" The religious question of modern times is: "What may I hope for?" This second question is very similar to the Jewish question. *The coming one* (*ho erchomenos*) was a symbol simultaneously for the messianic liberator and for God himself. Jesus' answer to John the Baptist's question was, as everyone knows, "Go and tell John what you see and hear: the blind see, the lame walk, lepers are cleansed and the deaf hear; the dead are raised up and the poor have the good news (gospel) proclaimed to them. And blessed is he who takes no offence at me (Matt 11:4–6). Similarly, Luke summarizes the messianic mission of Jesus: "The Spirit of the Lord is upon me to preach the good news to the poor, to heal the broken hearted, to proclaim release to the captives and recovery of sight to the blind, to set at liberty those who are oppressed, and to proclaim the acceptable (jubilee) year of the Lord." (Luke 4:18ff.) The universal question about the future concentrates here on the question of the "coming one" who will turn calamity to wholeness of salvation and lead people from oppression to freedom.

When Jesus shows himself to be *the coming one* through his gospel to the poor, his healing of the sick and his forgiveness of sinners, and when he is believed in and known as *the coming one* by those people who are affected, then the whole future of salvation and the kingdom of freedom must be expected from him. Where the poor hear the gospel through him, where the blind recover their sight through him, where the lame walk, where the oppressed are set free and sins are forgiven, there he reveals himself as the Christ because he makes present their true future.

Jesus' messianic message and deeds may be summarized by the concept of *eschatological anticipation*: through him and in his way "the kingdom of God has come near," so that already his healing, liberating and saving actions can be experienced now. We can therefore summarize the many diverse messianic titles found in the New Testament by saying: "Jesus-anticipator of the kingdom of God." But if Jesus is the *anticipator* of God then he must simultaneously and unavoidably become the sign of opposition to the powers of a world which is opposed to God and to this world's laws which are closed to the future. Because he proclaimed the kingdom of God to the poor he came into conflict with the rich. Because he gave the grace of God to sinners, he contradicted the laws of the pious, the Pharisees and the Zealots. Because he revealed God's lordship to the lowly and oppressed, Pilate let him be crucified in the name of the Roman Caesar-god.

Eschatological anticipation, thus inevitably brings forth historical resistance. Salvation can enter the situation of misery in no other way; liberation can enter into a world of oppression in no other way.

When we read again the story of Jesus in the light of his proclamation of the coming God, we know him much more clearly. Then we understand more clearly Jesus' resurrection from the dead: God raised him *from* the dead. This means that the universal resurrection of the dead has already begun in this one. The time of the end has already broken in. The future has already begun. Because people have faith in, and see the risen Christ, the people of the end-time unite together—as the body of the Messiah—in expectation of the coming kingdom of God. Jesus' resurrection from the dead must be understood as eschatological anticipation and promise, as the real beginning of the resurrection process and the world's new creation of the end-time (Rom 8:11). Thus in the New Testament the raised one is named "the first fruits of those who have fallen asleep" (1 Cor 15:20) and "the leader of life" (Acts 3:15). From this Easter sign and promise arises for Jesus' followers the unambiguous and definite hope for the coming kingdom; out of this stance of waiting and expectation comes also the practical passion to renew life now in the spirit of resurrection, and not to equate the messianic vision with the system of this world.

Indeed, this Easter anticipation is also related to resistance, namely to the cross of Christ and to the cross which Christians carry. Whom did God raise from the dead? Just any person? No, this particular one—the condemned blasphemer, the crucified rebel, the abandoned son of God. The future of God and of salvation—the kingdom of God and God's freedom for humanity—is therefore recognizable and realized in no place other than in the poor and violated Jesus, crucified for us.

This brings us then to the dialectic between the crucifixion and resurrection of Jesus Christ. For,

- by his suffering he freed the sufferers;
- by his weakness he wins power in the world;
- by his God-forsakenness he brings God to the forsaken and abandoned;
- by his death he creates salvation for those condemned to death.

The lordship of Christ is no royal, kingly lordship (Barth) but the lordship of the obedient servant of God (Philippians 2), the Lamb of God (Revelation)! Nor is the lordship of Christ a "religious rule," separated from the kingdom of the world; it is rather the rule of the real bodily crucified one in the midst of this world. He rules by serving. He redeems through suffering. He liberates through his sacrifice. The unity of the risen and the crucified one is grasped by neither a two kingdoms doctrine nor by the doctrine of the kingly lordship of Christ, but only by an eschatological Christology.

In saying this we are already exercising a friendly critique of both Luther and Barth, and in this way:

1. Although Luther related his theology of the cross critically to the church and to faith so that it was also liberating, he left the social and political consequences to Müntzer and others, whom he declared and condemned as "enthusiasts." In Protestantism that led to the result that the lordship of the crucified one is only to be interpreted for those justified by faith. Political theology, however, begins from the assumption that Christ was not crucified between two candles on an altar, nor that the effects of his death belong only to the privacy of the individual-personal life; rather, as Hebrews says, Jesus was led "outside" the gate of the city. The salvation which faith embraces in hope is therefore not a *private* but a *public* salvation, not only spiritual but also bodily, not a purely religious but also a political salvation. We may not separate this into two kingdoms but must recognize the form of the cross in this Savior and his salvation.

2. With his doctrine of the Pantokrator Christ, Barth, on the other side, fell into a kind of enthusiasm. But, as Hebrews says, "As it is, we do not yet see everything in subjection to him" (2:8). Ernest Käsemann described this Pauline "not-yet" the "eschatological reserve." Certainly the crucified one is already the Lord in his person, but he is, as such, still on the way to his kingdom. He draws the faithful into his way toward his Father. This conclusively

provisional character is the historical form of the lordship of the crucified one. The theology of the cross is always a theology of the way and, equally, the theology of the way is a theology of the cross. Thus the Christian hope leads to conflict, contradiction and suffering because it resists evil and everything which resists the coming of God's kingdom; it will become certain of victory only *in* this struggle, not apart from it, and certainly not in flight from it!

To sum up this section: political theology strongly appeals to its christological basis; it anticipates the coming of *the resurrected-crucified* Jesus. This anticipation, rooted in this particular cross-and-resurrection-messianism, leads the followers of Jesus into active struggle for the kingdom's victory coming into the world.

Political Hermeneutics

The eschatological hermeneutics of history

"Hermeneutics" signifies the art of interpretation of the witnesses of the past. Every interpretation has two sides, a historical and prophetic side; it includes historical explication and prophetic application: one must ascertain by means of historical-critical research what words, sentences, stories and symbols meant in their own time; one also must understand prophetically what they mean in our time. Hermeneutics is, therefore, the art of translation from the past into the present.

But why should we *re*-present the past by interpreting the witness to earlier events? Whence arises the interest which guides such knowledge? The past is not *re*-presented for the sake of its pure pastness. Only when something sticks in the past that points beyond itself into the future is there any point in remembering the past. The unfulfilled character of the past, its future-oriented direction and its original primal character, presses upon the present because it seeks its fulfillment and completion. Hermeneutics returns to the past because it seeks the future in this past. History is "hope in the mode of remembrance."

Christian hermeneutics then reads the Bible as the witness of God's history of promise and the human history of hope. Its "interest in leading to knowledge" is an interest in the power of the future and how this is revealed in God's promises and stirred in human hope. Because God's history of promise, about which the Bible in its core speaks, has liberated people from their inner and outer prisons ever anew—Israel from Egypt, Jesus from death, and the church from the nations, the remembrance of this story, therefore, is as dangerous as it is liberating for every present moment; the promise of hope in the crucified Christ is dangerous for the powerful, but liberating for the powerless. By looking backward from our present, to this story, we learn to see also beyond our own present into the future, promised by Christ and the Messianic kingdom. This then is the prophetic side of hermeneutics: "Past things become present in order to announce the things of the future" (Augustine).

In *World History and Salvation History* Karl Löwith called the historian a prophet who is turned backwards. We can expand this insight and call the prophet a historian who is turned towards the front. As the historian discovers hope in the mode of memory, so the prophet shapes memory in the mode of hope. For the "Power of the future," anticipated in the biblical history of promise, stretches far beyond the present and its given possibilities. To grasp this in hope means to become free. We then understand history as a whole as the element of the future. What we call *the past* are anticipations of the future which have preceded us. When we orient the present towards this future, it becomes a new front-line of this future. Then history is no longer the history of death and decay; it is rather the history of the future. When we speak in such an absolute and dominant way of *the future* which defines all history and therefore does not decay, *God* is meant as the "Power of the future." The power of his future affects people in such a way that they are liberated from the compulsion to repeat the past and from bondage to the givens of what is already there. To speak of the history of this future means to speak of the history of human liberation. That is the basic thinking then of the eschatologically oriented hermeneutic of history as it has developed through stimulation from Ernst Bloch.

Political hermeneutics: by participation in God's history, we learn to understand God's history

Political hermeneutics links up with eschatological hermeneutics. Early hermeneutics usually remained at one level: from manuscript to manuscript, from understanding to understanding, from faith to faith. When hermeneutics, however, involves a history of promise, then the way of translation goes from promise to fulfillment. When it involves a history of hope, then the way goes from exposition of the hope to realization. When it involves the hope of liberation, then the way goes from oppression to freedom: i.e., hermeneutics does not remain on the level of intellectual history nor on the theoretical level, but wants to lead, by way of the experience of understanding hope, to a new *praxis* of hope. In this regard, the thesis of Karl Marx is pertinent: "The philosophers have only differently interpreted the world, whereas everything depends upon transforming it."

When the remembered promises press for the liberation of people and for the humanizing of their relationships, the reverse of this thesis is true: everything depends upon interpreting these transformations critically. The way of political hermeneutics cannot go one-sidedly from reflection to action. That would be pure idealism. The resulting action would become blind. Instead, this hermeneutic must bind reflection and action together, thus requiring reflection in the action as well as action in the reflection. The hermeneutical method to which this leads is called in the ecumenical discussion: "the action-reflection method." Christian hope motivates those who hope for the liberating act of love; the historical practice of liberation, however, must be reflected upon in the light of this hope, and criticized in its effects and consequences.

To say this differently: without personal participation in the apostolic mission and without cooperation with the kingdom of God, one cannot understand the Bible. And without understanding the Bible, one cannot participate in the mission of the apostolate, nor can one cooperate with the kingdom of God in the world. Political hermeneutics leads to experiences in Christian passion and action. In political activity and suffering one begins to read the Bible with the eyes of the poor, the oppressed and the guilty—and to understand it.

Political hermeneutics therefore rejects pure theory in theology just as it does blind activism in ethics. Its model is a differentiated theory-praxis relationship in which theory and praxis, thinking and doing, mutually drive each other forward. Theory and practice do not belong in two different kingdoms; however, they are never totally equivalent. They do not come to a unity in history. They constantly overlap so that theory must subsume practice and practice must incorporate theory. By means of critical theory one frees oneself from previous practice and pushes toward new liberating experience. In critical praxis one follows a theory and, through new experiences, evaluates and possibly transforms it. Such a theory then does not restrict itself to world thought but attempts to understand itself as a moment in the process by which the world will be transformed—because it opens itself to the future of the kingdom of God.

The Ethics of Hope: Resistance and Anticipation

The political ethic which results from the Lutheran two kingdoms theory is an inherently secular, realistic and conservative ethic. It wishes to see the present orders of state and society as "God's ordinances" and seeks to exercise love within them (Augs. Conf., 16). Its aim is the preservation of the world against threatening chaos "until that lovely last day," but not the anticipatory realization of the kingdom of God on earth. Conversely, the political ethics which follows from Barth's doctrine of the lordship of Christ seeks a way between the strict separation of the world and the kingdom of God. Rather than accepting an easy identification of the world with the kingdom of God, it seeks to relate these two with parables, hints and signs; these point to the kingdom of God in history.

The political ethic which follows from political theology begins with Barth's emphasis, but also goes beyond it. Barth's political parables, images and analogies in the civil community are answers to the already completed salvation event in Christ; the Christian community, therefore, is a prototype. But when one begins with the eschatological Christology presented here and understands history as the history of God's future, then these political parables and social analogies have not only a responsive or corresponding character turned backwards; they possess also simultaneously a character of anticipation which is directed forwards.

Because the congregation attempts to correspond to Christ as messianic Lord also in political and social activity, it anticipates in history the kingdom of God.

These anticipations are not yet the kingdom of God itself. But they are real mediations of the kingdom of God within the limited possibilities of history. They are, to speak with Paul, a pledge (*arrabōn*) and the first fruits (*aparchē*) of God's kingdom in the midst of human history. This ethic then is christologically founded, eschatologically oriented and pneumatologically implemented. This world is not a "waiting room for the kingdom of God." Though this world is not yet the kingdom of God itself, it is the battleground and the construction site for the kingdom, which comes from God onto the earth. We can already live now in the Spirit of this kingdom through new obedience and creative discipleship. But as long as the dead are dead and we cannot achieve justice for humanity, love remains fragmentary.

Furthermore, the Pauline ethic participates in the sacramental nature of early Christian baptism and eucharistic celebration; it is a sacramental ethic. The church, its proclamation, baptism, and the Eucharist are not themselves already the kingdom of God, but they make the kingdom present in a sacramental way. When Barth speaks of ethics in parables, signs and analogies for the kingdom of God, this is also sacramental language. His ethic corresponds to his doctrine of baptism. For the mediation of the future kingdom into history completes itself "Christianly" by means of the sacraments. Christian ethics, therefore, also makes the future of the kingdom present in a corresponding way. When ethics is understood in this way, however, it is not sufficient to see in liberating and healing acts simply a parable, only a sign and only a hint of the freedom and salvation of the kingdom. We must go a step further then and discover the unconditioned within the conditioned, the last in the next to last and the eschatological in the ethical, just as we believe that the blood and body of Christ is present in the bread and wine of the Eucharist. In the sacrament of Christian ethics, we experience the *real* history, for the ethic is the element of the kingdom of God coming into the material of our history. Christian praxis—in its suffering, struggle, and hope—celebrates and completes then the presence of God in history.

The human person is not a one-dimensional being. He/she always lives and suffers simultaneously in many different dimensions. Christian-messianic activity, therefore, can also not proceed mono-dimensionally but must participate in complex interrelated historical processes and the many dimensions of human experience. I will identify here the fundamental dimensions in which messianic activity must take place today:

1. The struggle for economic justice against the exploitation of some people by other people.
2. The struggle for human rights and freedom against the political oppression of some people by other people (be it patriarchalism, nationalism, or other such isms).
3. The struggle for human solidarity against the cultural alienation of people from people.
4. The struggle for ecological peace with nature against the industrial destruction of nature by humans.
5. The struggle for the meaning of life against apathy in personal life.

These five dimensions, in which messianic activity is needed, hang so closely together that one cannot be without the others; there can be no economic justice without political freedom, no improvement of socio-economic conditions without the conquering of cultural alienation, and no ecological peace or economic justice without personal conversion from apathy to hope. Whoever does not understand salvation in this "catholic" sense and does not strive for this comprehensive anticipation, does not understand salvation holistically.

Epilogue

Christian messianic ethics celebrates and anticipates the presence of God in history. It wants to practice the unconditioned within the conditioned and the last things in the next to last. In the economic dimension, God is present in bread; in healing, as health. In the political dimension God is present as the dignity of the human being; in the cultural dimension, as solidarity. In the ecological area, God is present as peace with nature; in the personal area, in the certainty of the heart. Every form of his presence is veiled and sacramental; it is not yet a presence face-to-face. God's presence encounters human persons in the concrete messianic form of his liberation from hunger, oppression, alienation, enmity and despair. These messianic forms of his presence point at the same time, however, beyond themselves to a greater presence, and finally to that present in which "God will be all in all."

God's real presence as bread, as freedom, as community, as peace and as certainty thus has the character of exploding the present. To act ethically in a Christian sense means to participate in God's history in the midst of our own history, to participate in the comprehensive process of God's liberation of the world, and to discover our own role in this, according to our own calling and abilities. A messianic ethic makes people into co-operators for the kingdom of God. It assumes that the kingdom of God is already here in concrete, if hidden, form. Messianic ethics integrates suffering people into God's history in this world; it is fulfilled by the hope of the completion of God's history in the world by God himself.

Messianic ethics makes everyday life into a feast of God's rule, just as Jesus did. The messianic feast becomes everyday life. As Athanasius once said, "the resurrected Christ makes life a feast, a feast without end." As we celebrate the presence of God's kingdom by identifying with and serving the needs of the poor, the downtrodden, the lonely, and the powerless, Christian ethics becomes a sacrament. Then in our normal daily life in the world, politics becomes worship (Rom 12:1–2).

4

Following Jesus Christ in an Age of Nuclear War

Context

In this last lecture I would like to explain the theological and ethical implications of the debate about armament and nuclear armament in Germany. I am speaking out of my situation and you must discern how to translate this into your situation. I do not claim to teach you what you should do in your situation; I have a hard time to find out what to do in my situation.

I am convinced that peace is a major theological problem of politics in this decade, just as unemployment is a major theological problem of our social situation. We all believe that God's peace is in heaven and on earth, but what is it and what does it mean for peacemaking on a violent earth? Shall we follow the radical discipleship of Christ? If we do so, do we abandon our responsibility for the world? We have on the one hand, especially in this seminary here, an old traditional peace church. My church, the Reformed Church, was called in history a traditional just war church. The question I face: can I still live with this tradition in my situation?

49

How is the situation in Europe today? I go back into history and read about three periods. We had in the 50's a peace movement under the slogan "Ban the Bomb." This was a time of the cold war in Europe, the Korean War in Asia, and the Berlin crisis in Europe. There was a confrontation building up in Europe and we had this peace movement "Ban the Bomb." But this was a voluntary movement, a voluntary group. This peace movement of the 50's waned when the time of a political peace policy came in the 60's. The treaties of the West German government with the USSR, Poland and East European countries brought us from a peace movement to the hope for a real peace policy in Europe. So in the 60's and 70's there was no considerable peace movement in my country but a real hope for peace policies, a detenté policy.

This changed dramatically when President Reagan and his administration came into office and a new conservative policy came out of the United States of America two years ago. The year 1981 was the year of the mushrooming of a European peace movement, a real nonviolent peaceful movement. The gathering on October 10 last year brought more than 300,000 young, but not only young, people to Bonn. When President Reagan visited us in June this year, 400,000 met on the other side of the Rhine. And this was also an unorganized and nonviolent gathering of people demonstrating for peace. And the beginning of this year showed us how an American peace movement also came into being; we have felt great support from the American peace movement.

This peace movement, in Europe and America is especially important to us because we live under the threat of Russia SS20 missiles in Europe. We were used to living under this threat already for a couple of years. But then we heard from the White House and the Pentagon about a public calculating of a limited nuclear war in Europe. All of a sudden my people got the feeling that our lives were at stake; a limited nuclear war in Europe must be in central Europe, and that is in the two parts of Germany, and we will be the first. Therefore the new peace movement in my country is not only a movement of young people. Many older people have joined the peace movement because they all fear the danger now at hand. So the character of the peace movement in Germany at the moment is a real peoples movement, not only a students movement. It is a Christian movement and not a Communist movement. The organizers of the great gathering in Bonn were two Christian organizations and no communist organizations. There is a small number of communists in the peace movement, but that doesn't matter.

This peace movement is important also because, for the first time, West Germany and East Germany are experiencing the same thing. We have had an autonomous peace movement of young Christian people in East Germany and they have a special difficulty because the policy of the DDR was always called, from the beginning, a peace policy. So they have had peace missiles and peace tanks; everything is for peace there. To create then an autonomous peace movement in such a situation has been especially difficult. But for the first time it has happened.

One must say that this is not only a crisis of military policy, but a crisis of the whole political industrial system—East and West. The armaments race in the north and the growing poverty in the south of the world belong together. We are destroying the third world more and more with our armaments race; the two developments are intertwined.

The question we face is: can a church as a whole become a peace church, or is this limited to only committed Christian groups in a church? We face also a related question: responsible support of the world orders of economics, society, culture and politics or consistent, undivided discipleship of Christ *in* economic, social, cultural and political conditions? This is the question today in view of the growing number of nuclear plants, further economic growth at the cost of poor peoples and the preparation for nuclear warfare. Should we boycott nuclear energy? Must we come up with alternative economic systems? Should we "live without armaments?" Can we afford to buy "no products of apartheid?" Or is it the case that we may not and cannot "drop out" and must therefore exist responsibly with nuclear energy, live with the bomb and use our economic relationships with South Africa to improve the conditions of the blacks there? Where are the limits of Christian responsible political engagement?

Christian Responsibility for the World or Discipleship of Christ? Reformation Reflections

Responsible participation or undivided discipleship? That was the question which stood behind the consequential and controversial Article 16 of the Augsburg Confession. Unfortunately it is not clearly recognizable and therefore overlooked by many that the Lutheran Church on *this* question took an unambiguous but also *one-sided* position. The reason for this was that with this confession at the Augsburg Reichstag the Protestants wanted to enter into discussion with the Emperor and Rome, but not with the "Left Wing of the Reformation," which was at that time still a widespread Anabaptist movement prepared for peace. Together with the Catholic Church the Protestants united themselves in a common condemnation and persecution of the Anabaptists. Who were the Anabaptists and what did they teach?

Article 16 of the *Confessio Augustana* is an answer to Article 6 of the *Schleitheim Articles of 1527* (the "Brotherly Union"), which Michael Sattler drafted for the first Anabaptist synod. Within a year (four months actually) Sattler was burned at the stake in nearby Rottenburg-am-Neckar. We begin with a systematic comparison of these two articles.

"The sword is a divine order outside of the perfection of the Christ" (Schleitheim Article 6).

This sentence summarizes the lived witness of the Anabaptists. The perfection of Christ can only be lived in the consistent and *undivided discipleship of Jesus.* This means that a Christian cannot serve two lords. If a person confesses "Christ alone:" as his or her Lord, then he or she must live solely according to the wisdom of Christ as it is expressed for the life of discipleship in the Sermon on the Mount. A Christian is not a person with a divided conscience. Therefore a Christian cannot commit an act of violence, not even to impede or punish others doing violent acts. It follows that a Christian cannot accept and practice a calling in economics and politics; this would compromise his or her faith by forcing him or her to use violence. For the Anabaptists of that time this meant no participation in public affairs which necessitated the use of the sword; hence this meant refusal to participate in the army, serve in the police functions, or hold positions in the court and the state.

The perfection of Christ can only be lived in the *voluntary community of brothers and sisters.* The voluntary community which is constituted by faith, discipleship and baptism is the true, visible body of Christ. In this visible community of believers there is only admonishment—no force, only forgiveness; no judgment, only love; no calculation, only obedience.

This voluntary community which is constituted by faith, discipleship and baptism is the true, visible body of Christ. This voluntary community of Christ is the visible *alternative* to the society of laws and compulsions: "It shall not be so among you . . ." (Matt 20:26ff). Many Anabaptists demonstrated this alternative in their own life communities: the Hutterite Brothers from Mähren created the "Brüderhöfe," which still exist in the United States and Canada. The Mennonites founded their own village communities in Russia, Paraguay and the United States. The current movement of basic communities and alternative rural communities on the land has Anabaptist origins.

The perfection of Christ is proven through the *refusal of participation in state acts of violence*. The Christian's ministry of peace demands the consistent *defenselessness* of life. The Anabaptists did not believe with Luther that executioners and soldiers could be in a "holy station," they refused participation in such public offices which "necessarily force one to sin." They refused to take oaths and repudiated that private ownership of land and tools which made other human beings into slaves.

Finally, the perfection of Christ can be witnessed in this violent world only through fundamental readiness and willingness for suffering and defenseless martyrdom. Patience, tolerance and "forbearance" were considered signs of the true church. Indeed the Anabaptists are the martyrs of the Reformation times—persecuted, condemned and executed by Protestants and Catholics alike. The *Book of Martyrs* and the moving Anabaptist song of 1527, "How precious is the consecrated death . . . ," speak a most impressive language. When Michael Sattler was interrogated at Rottenburg about how to defend against the danger of the Turks stirring out of the East, he replied, "Live defenseless!"

Love of neighbor, defenselessness, readiness for suffering are for the "Anabaptist" the signs of discipleship of Christ based on personal faith and one's own decision. Is this responsible Christian existence? There remain open questions. The "community of Christ" and "this world" stand in exclusive opposition. Only in apocalyptic times has the Christian community experienced such alternatives. From this perspective the community of Christ must separate itself from "this world." Is "this world" thus lost? Is this world, despite its violence and inhumanity, not God's good creation? If the community of Christ separates itself from society, does it not then show only its own "great refusal," but not the criticism of this violent world in light of the judgment and kingdom of God?

"... *all established rule and laws were instituted and ordained by God* ..."
(*Confessio Augustana*, Article 16).

This sentence appropriately summarizes the witness of the "Lutheran responsibility for the world." If all established rule is *from God*, then the participation of Christians in ruling offices and their conduct according to public laws cannot as such be considered sinful. To civil offices and to actions according to public laws also belongs the Christian's right to "render decisions and pass sentence according to imperial and other existing laws, punish evil doers with the sword, engage in just wars, serve as soldiers, buy and sell, take required oaths, possess property, be married, etc." None of this contradicts the gospel because the gospel teaches an "eternal righteousness in the heart." The perfection of Christ is not external, but rather internal. It is the "proper fear of God and real faith in God." Because "the gospel does not teach an outward and temporal but an inward and eternal mode of existence and the righteousness of the heart," it does not overturn the worldly regiment but requires that the political and economic orders be kept as "true orders of God" (*Conservare tamquam ordinationes Dei*) and that love be practiced *in* these orders. Thus Christians are obliged to be subject to civil authority and obey its commands and laws. Fortunately, the Augsburg Confession also added a phrase at the end of this wholesale declaration of civil authorities, namely, "except when they command to sin" (*nisi cum jubent peccare*). "When commands of the civil authority cannot be obeyed without sin, we must obey God rather than men," says Article 16.

We have here in classical form the basic ideas of Christian responsibility for the world: every political power contains an element of "good order" without which there can be no common human life. Civil authority is created by God and equipped with a monopoly of force so that social peace might be preserved and political justice established. It belongs to Christians as such to respect and responsibly maintain civil authority. The political obligation of Christians is not the "great refusal" but responsible cooperation.

But according to which criteria should Christians cooperate? The gospel, they believe, offers no new perspectives for the transformation of structures but rather only obligates Christians to "love *in* structures." Love penetrates all political and economic orders but does not transform them. It presupposes that in the normal situation God speaks through the gospel internally in the heart with the same language with which the authorities created and set in place by God speak externally. In cases of doubt one must obey God more than human beings, that is, the gospel more than the authorities.

But if Christian world responsibility means leading a responsible life *in* the world orders, then this means that God, not the human being, is responsible for it. Christian responsibility for the world thereby gains a fundamentally preserving tendency: against the temptation to disintegrate (*dissipare*) political and economic orders, it conserves them by explaining them as "God's orders." This conservative orientation is grounded in the faith that the preservation of the world by the divinely ordained authorities is willed by God until the end of time (*conservatio mundi*). The criteria for Christian responsibility for the world are thus love and reason. There is no such thing as a peculiarly Christian view of justice or a wisdom which is specifically Christian. This formulation of Christian responsibility for the world makes the Christian unrecognizable in worldly callings and positions, for in ordinary situations he/she chooses to do exactly the same thing that non-Christians do.

The critical questions which arise here are numerous: If the gospel really teaches only the righteousness of the heart, then the thought of the actually lived, incarnated—that is, also political and economic—discipleship is sacrificed. A faith which is made so internal delivers over the external world to other powers which it must then explain as divine orders; these then must be obeyed, but "without sin." But can just any group—militaristic and even terrorist perhaps—who come to power by the use of arms be regarded as a divine order? Should the text be understood to say "all authorities," or only legitimate governments (*legitimas ordinationes*), as the Latin says.

So just as the Anabaptists stand in danger of pulling themselves back out of the world as quietists and thus without criticism, so the Lutherans stand in danger of going along with the world as it is and cooperating without criticism. The "silent ones in the land" and the "pious state underlings" thus in the end have little to contribute to peace and justice in economics and politics in the world.

Further, this conflict of the Lutherans and the Anabaptists over responsible participation or undivided discipleship provides no direct way to address the problems of Christian witness in the nuclear age. However, for Christians today the patterns of both of these decisions are always close at hand. These great alternatives constantly obtrude in many individual decisions; the basic thinking for these decisions remains similar to that of the sixteenth century.

"Justified Nuclear War" or "Refusal of Nuclear Weapons"?

We begin with the major pronouncements of the Reformed Church of the Netherlands (1962, 1978), of the Protestant Church in Germany (1969, 1981), and of the Reformed Alliance in Germany (1982). According to these pronouncements we must assume that *peace* is the order and promise of God: God wants to live with human beings in a kingdom of peace. Because of this the people of God are given their *task of peace*. Peace means not only the absence of war but also the overcoming of suffering, anxiety, threat, injustice, and oppression. Peace is the blessed, affirmed, good, splendid life with God, with human beings, and with nature: *Shalom*. It is the commission of Christians to serve this peace in all dimensions of life, to promote it and protect it, but in particular to resist war, the most dangerous form of the lack of peace. Christian churches have always viewed their position against war as only one part of their comprehensive service of peace.

In view of the fact and possibility of war there have been among Christians two different approaches:

Principled pacifism (from the traditional peace churches). This approach refuses every act of violence, including those acts of violence by which violence is to be prevented. Here the discipleship of Christ is given priority over political responsibility for one's own people. The responsibility for the consequences of this discipleship is given over to God: "Do not have anxiety . . ."

56

The doctrine of "just war." Whoever is not a pacifist always explains himself/herself with a kind of "doctrine of just war." This doctrine does not intend to provide a justification for war—we must be clear about this—but seeks to apply the moral criteria of justice and injustice to the conduct of war. With this doctrine the moral norms of good and evil are applied to the execution of war. According to this theory war must be conceived as a means of politics or a continuation of politics by other means. Yet we should be aware of the fact that the doctrine of the "just war" was not developed for the justification of war but for the limitation of war, because no one is allowed to participate in an unjust war (both the Vietnam war and the Falkland's war, e.g., were, according to this tradition, unjust wars because war was never declared).

The decisive elements of the doctrine of the "just war" are:

1. War must be declared by a legitimate authority; it must serve the common good of the state.
2. It must be conducted with a good intention.
3. It must be conducted with the expectation of a good outcome: the general situation after the war must be better than the situation before it.
4. All peaceful means for a resolution of the conflict must have been exhausted.
5. The means of the war may not be worse than the evil which is supposed to be overcome by it, that is, the means must stand in the right relationship to the end.
6. There must be a distinction between soldiers and citizens. The civil population must be protected.

Points 1–4 relate to *jus ad bellum,* (the right to war); point 6 to *jus in bello* (justice in war) and point 5 relates to both. Those who find these considerations somewhat macabre in the world today may apply these points to a doctrine of the "just liberation struggle" and think, for example, about the struggle of the Sandinistas against Samosa in Nicaragua. But we in the Federal Republic of Germany have to come to grips with the possession of nuclear weapons, and now, quite specifically, the refusal of armament or disarmament; we must in this situation live out our service of peace as Christians and churches of Christ. Our efforts to find the right way have taken place within the context of five related considerations, in the church and in the world generally:

The Doctrine of the "Just Nuclear War"

According to this doctrine nuclear war is not to be directly justified but rather confined to prescribed limits. The possession of weapons is not refused. Having weapons is part of the present deterrent system which "secures peace." The use of the weapons is subjected to the norm of the appropriateness of the means and the norm of the differentiation between military and civilian population. This means that the massive destruction of large cities is not allowed; only the selective use on military objectives is allowed. The strategy of "massive retaliation," therefore, is not to be justified. As a result of the strategic attacks on military installations, however, civil population will be destroyed, and this is inevitable. This inevitability is thus a part of the deterrence strategy because it provides an additional threat to the opponent. But mass destruction cannot be espoused. Hence it is prohibited to be the first one to use nuclear weapons. If this is prohibited, then it is also prohibited to prepare for a first-strike capacity. These considerations, arising from the application of the just war theory, do not exclude, however—to this point in the discussion— nuclear armament as such.

By its further development of nuclear weapons the government of the United States (and the USSR as well) is obviously following the position of "just nuclear war": the neutron bomb, the Pershing II and the Cruise missiles can be employed with precision against military objectives without causing massive destruction of civil population. Out of the old strategy of massive destruction has developed the more finely tuned strategy of "limited nuclear war." Nuclear weapons are thus *made useable.* Accordingly, the process of increasing armaments is organized more and more. With this, however, the threshold of the beginning of a nuclear war has come only considerably nearer. And because no one knows whether a "limited nuclear war" can be kept within limits, the situation in Europe has become not more secure but less secure. As far as I am aware, no one in our European churches is a proponent of a "just nuclear war," because the limiting of such a war cannot be assured.

The Doctrine of the "Just Nuclear Armament"

While the doctrine of the "just nuclear war" has been refused, the doctrine of "just nuclear armament," however, is maintained in both pronouncements of the Protestant church of Germany (EKD) of which we have spoken (1969, 1981): By means of the parity of armaments the present "peace" is preserved; only a situation of parity will allow negotiations for disarmament; and, further, the mutually incredible horror of attack prevents a nuclear war. Because disarmament steps can be taken only on the basis of military parity, armaments must be increased. But this can be justified only if the "breathing space" or "grace period" is used to move from armed peace to a security system without nuclear weapons and to build an international order of peace.

According to this doctrine, therefore, only the *possession* and *threat*, but not the *use* of nuclear weapons, may be allowed. If, however, one is not ready to use what one possesses, no deterrence results. To this extent there is an illusion here. On the other hand, it was already recognized in the 1969 pronouncement: "The expectations which in the early 1960's were connected with international politics on the basis of "armament control" can no longer be maintained." The "breathing space" or "grace period" was not used for peace—not because of bad will, but because the possibility did not actually exist: In the midst of the armaments race one can hardly speak of disarmament. The speed of increased armaments is always many times greater than the speed of disarmament talks (compare, e.g., the relationship between the Geneva talks to limit intermediate-range missiles while at the same time development plans proceed for space war missiles!).

The Apocalyptic Threshold

Among many people today the impression is growing that increased armaments of nuclear weapons do not secure peace but rather lead more and more into a collective insanity. The deterrent systems have their own laws. Within their logic it is not asked whether something serves peace and life but whether it increases the enemy's fear of one's own strike capacity. Kurt Biedenkopf is right when he calls "peace" based on nuclear deterrence an "ultimate threshold," because nuclear deterrence presents the threat of the enemy as world destruction. A securing of "peace" by means of threatening world destruction can never be stabilized as a permanent condition. This situation is therefore unsuitable as the foundation of a permanent order of peace. That an apocalyptic peace of deterrence is not even "capable of gaining democratic consensus" shows that among the peoples of the world there is still a healthy human understanding.

There is ethically no conceivable justification of a possible destruction of humanity and of life on earth in order to protect the rights and freedom in one of the social systems in which human beings live today. A "peace" which is bought with the threat of world destruction is no peace. The peace of deterrence through mutual fear may technically be "non-employment of weapons," but it is not peace. Mutual deterrence through fear is a condition of extreme lack of peace, because it increases potential realities of violence. Even without nuclear war the stock-piling of armaments already destroys the life of human beings and the natural environment. The "military-industrial complex" spreads itself like a cancerous growth and infects all dimensions of life. Unnoticed, a total mobilization has come into being.

We call, therefore, for "withdrawal from the apocalyptic threshold," a gradual nuclear disengagement as a first step and then the gradual dismantling of conventional armaments. But is such a withdrawal still at all possible? Does not the turning back away from an apocalyptic death zone unto life mean a comprehensive transformation of the whole system in which we live? If for a moment we imagine that the nuclear threat did not exist, we would then have to disband the military, dismantle the armaments industry, establish the state economy without a military budget, free our souls from anxiety and aggression, and . . . But because this idea sounds so utopian, it is clear that we have never thought through it seriously; this shows that we quite pessimistically believe that the "point of no return" has already been reached and we have become prisoners of the deterrence system. In terms of political rhetoric the "force of the issue" and the "momentum" have already taken the place of free, responsible decisions.

"To Live Without Armaments"

A person who recognizes that mutual deterrence through fear is based not on a parity of armaments but on an armaments race which is already now bleeding the nations to death and can lead to no good end stands before the decision either to go along with it or to protest against it. It is therefore understandable that the old movement which worked under the slogan "Ban the Bomb," a "struggle against nuclear death," is being resurrected in Europe today under the self-obligating formulation "live without armaments" (*Ohne Rüstung Leben*) The logic is clear: The use of nuclear weapons is irresponsible and sin.

But if the use is irresponsible and sin then the possession also can not be considered responsible, for the possession binds the possessor to rearmament, improved rearmament, modernization, etc., and also, in the long run, to their use. If, however, the possession is not to be considered responsible, then one must withdraw from the universal arms race and devote all of one's efforts to an alternative service of peace just as the Anabaptists and Mennonites who were prepared for peace have done for a long time—and this was written not simply for this occasion of dialogue here.

"To live without armaments" can have two dimensions, a personal and a political dimension.

First, Christians who place the discipleship of Christ over responsibility for the world can deny themselves without making their own denial a model and a law for all human beings, Christians and non-Christians. That was the way of the Anabaptists: Defenselessness, bound with the readiness for suffering and martyrdom, is the way of faith, and this faith is "not everyone's thing" (we can expect it from those who believe, but not from those who do not have the strength of faith; it is a personal commitment, but not a political proposal).

Second, Christians and non-Christians who want to end the arms race can deny themselves and make their readiness to live without armament a political injunction for all human beings of their nation.

In the first case the risk is personal; in the second case it is also political. In the first case one takes the consequences upon oneself; in the second case one must think of the consequences for others.

Wherein does the risk lie in the second case? Whoever disarms unilaterally and brings to the enemy preliminary achievements for peace can of course by this very action provoke the foe to aggression (e.g., it is sometimes said that England and France's peace initiative in 1939 provoked Hitler's aggression). Even if no aggression results, one can thereby become subject to black-mailing and extortion through the threats of the adversary. In this way one delivers oneself and one's own to the more powerful foe. Therefore whoever believes that nuclear war can be prevented only through unilateral disarmament must be ready to sacrifice not only himself or herself but also his or her own people. Such a person must risk the freedom, the rights and the security of his or her own country in order to save the whole of life on this earth from nuclear death. Therefore, a more conservative group in the European church says that the slogan, "live without armament," serves not the resistance but the intensification of military practices in world politics" ("Sicherung des Friedens," 1980, Thesis 9). To be sure, this risk is not yet provable because as of yet no one has made the experiment, but it is a fear which cannot easily be laid to rest as long as the adversary is believed to be capable only of the worst, but not of the rational. And this leads to the controversy of what we, the West, can expect of the Russians—the worst or the rational.

"Complementarity"

In and of themselves the two basic decisions, "just nuclear armament" and "refusal of nuclear weapons," contradict each other. The EKD pronouncements (1969, 1981), however, recommend a third, combined standpoint. It is the thesis of the complementarity of both decisions which, just as much as they mutually exclude each other, also limit, and in view of the common goal of peace, even complete each other. Out of this idea, then, has been developed the formula of "service of peace with and without weapons." The "service of peace without weapons" is not seen as "alternative service" but as directed toward the "goal of international solidarity." It should be possible for an individual to engage in the "service of peace without weapons" in place of his military service "but without thereby forcing him to a decision of conscience against military service," says the pronouncement of 1969. If the "service of peace without weapons" did not exist, then the armament would become total and without limits. If the "service of peace with weapons" did not exist, then the "service of peace without weapons" would be overcome by the weapons of the foe. But this complementarity is illuminating only so long as military armament has the goal of preventing nuclear warfare in order to gain time for building another system of peace. But that is an illusion. The complementarity thesis does not remove the personal decisions of any Christian, for no one can decide complementarity. This is a position of church leaders who believe that they must always stand "for everyone." But it cannot be the position of Christian persons who must decide this way or that.

Remembering the Sermon on the Mount

Up to now both sides of this issue have made their calculations as if neither Christ nor the Sermon on the Mount existed. With Christ, however, there comes into the calculation a factor which suspends the whole process and changes everything: It is the *reality of God* which actually supports us all.

"You are children of your Father in heaven," says Jesus. This remembrance calls us out of the conflict. Whoever engages in a struggle and arbitrates a conflict stands under the law of retaliation. Otherwise the parity in the conflict cannot be maintained: eye for an eye, tooth for a tooth, armament-counterarmament, proliferation-counterproliferation. When we engage an enemy on the basis of the law of retaliation, however, we enter into a vicious circle from which we can no longer escape. We become enemy to our enemy and horrified by our own fear. We threaten what threatens us and we hate what hates us. We are more and more determined by the enemy. When evil is retaliated with evil, then there arises one evil after another, and that is deadly. We can be freed from such vicious circles only when our orientation to the foe ceases and another one becomes more important to us.

The love which Jesus puts in place of retaliation is the love of the enemy. The love of friends, "mutual love," is nothing special" it is only retaliation of good with good. The love of the enemy, however, is not recompensing, but is rather an anticipating, intelligent, and creative love. Whoever repays evil with good must be really free, strong and sovereign. The love for the enemy does not mean surrender to the enemy, submission to his will. For rather, he or she is no longer in the stance of reacting to the enemy, but seeks to create something new, a new situation for the enemy and for himself/herself. He/she follows his/her own intention and no longer allows the law of actions to be prescribed by the foe. Jesus did not die with a curse upon his enemies but rather with a prayer for them. In his life, his passion and his dying Jesus revealed the perfection of God: "Be perfect, even as your heavenly Father is perfect."

Of what does God's perfection consist? In no way is a moral perfectionism meant. It consists of that love which is long-suffering, friendly and patient, which does not add to evil or carry a grudge, which bears all things, believes all things and hopes all things (1 Corinthians 13). God's perfection lies in the fact that he loves his enemies, blesses them, does good to them and does not return evil for their evil. It is precisely from this that we all live. The whole world lives from this divine reality, even if it does not know it. As Jesus said, God is like the sun rising on the evil and the good, or like the rain pouring down upon the just and the unjust. Hence God bears all and maintains all because he hopes for each one. God's perfection is his limitless ability for suffering, his almightiness is his patient suffering for and with all things. God's uniqueness is his inexhaustible creative power of love.

In former times, we have asked only: What serves our security, what serves our survival? But now in listening to the Sermon on the Mount and seeking to experience God's love for the enemy, we must rephrase the basic question: What is the most helpful thing for "the enemy?" In what way can we best bless those who curse us? How do we do good for those who hate us? To remain concrete for my situation in Germany; since we Germans fear the Russians (and otherwise almost nothing on the face of the earth), we must ask: What helps the Russian people to gain peace more, our further armament or our disarmament? In what way can we bless the communist who curses us? In what way can we do good for the peoples of the "third world" who consider us their exploiter and enemy?

The politics of "national security" is, to a large degree, a politics of anxiety and fear: Because we have anxiety we demand security. Because we demand security, we increase our armaments. As we increase our arms we give terror to our adversary. Therefore our adversary also increases his arms. Quite to the contrary of this system, creative intelligent love arises out of freedom, out of the freedom to be a child of the eternal God, and that means out of the freedom from the fear of temporal death. Out of this freedom can come love for the enemy and the work for peace. Can one, however, really become free from this anxiety? One can become at least a bit freer from it when one recognizes the danger and consciously enters into the risk. To the degree that the risk of the vulnerable, defenseless but creative life becomes conscious to us, the more free and patient we become. Only the unknown and the repressed make us really anxious. In this sense I am personally willing and ready to live without armaments.

The Consequence: To Proclaim Peace

I come now to the 1981 Declaration on Peace by the Society of Protestant Theology (of which I have been president since 1981) and the statement of the Reformed Alliance in Germany from August, 1982. These two groups have made clear statements against nuclear war and armament and for disarmament. What follows represents, first, the Declaration of 1981.

> Jesus Christ, as he is witnessed to us in the Holy Scriptures and lives among us in the Holy Spirit, is *our peace* (Eph 2:14). In him the eternal God has reconciled the world with himself (2 Cor 5:14). Through him the world will be redeemed. Through the gospel he makes his peace to be proclaimed among us (Eph 6:15).

There are no dimensions of our life in which we cannot be certain of the peace of God. There are no conflicts in our life, neither personal nor political, which are not embraced by God's will for peace with human beings and his whole creation. There are no enemies, neither personal nor political, for whom God's will for peace does not apply.

We deny God's peace when we secure ourselves before our enemies by becoming enemies to them, when we encounter their threat with counter-threat and their terror with horror. God's peace rather makes it possible for us to *love our enemies creatively* by understanding their suffering, by thinking through our own position critically, and by making every conceivable effort to dismantle their and our enmity. Love of the enemy is an expression of the sovereign *freedom of the children of God* and has nothing to do with weakness and submission.

From the modern, military *means of mass destruction* comes not only a *deadly danger* for humanity and all life on earth; it threatens us also with *immeasurable guilt* (and this reflects our experience as German Christians from WW II, after which we must ask how we can come to the judgment of God).

The Reformed Declaration says:

Jesus Christ is our peace. By reconciling the world to God upon his cross he made peace between man, God's enemy and God. To him as the risen and ascended Lord belongs all power on heaven and on earth. He has sent his community into the world to witness to his peace, to spread the word of reconciliation and, in obedience to the word, to live in peace. His peace which the world can neither give, secure, nor destroy sets us free to pray, to think and to work for peace among men.

This confession of our faith is incompatible with the opinion that the question of peace on earth among men is simply a matter of political calculation and, accordingly, to be settled independently of the challenge and claim of the gospel's embassy for peace. In the face of the threat to peace posed by the means of mass destruction by both conventional weapons of mass destruction and A, B and C weapons, we as a church have often kept silent for too long or not witnessed to the will of the Lord with sufficient decision. Now as the possibility of atomic war is becoming a probability, we come to this recognition: the issue of peace is a confessional issue. In our opinion the *status confessionis* is given to it because the attitude taken toward mass destruction has to do with the affirmation or denial of the gospel itself.

Now these are the first two clear statements of official churches in my country. It is instructive to compare these statements with the Declaration of the Brethren, from 1958:

The deployment of means of mass destruction in the use of the state's threat of power and use of power can only result in the factual denial of

God's gracious will for his creation and for human beings. Such conduct simply cannot be represented as Christian. To maintain a position of neutrality on this stance, which is recognized as sinful by us, cannot be harmonized with the confession of Jesus Christ.

To conclude this presentation, I explicate further the convictions of these statements, and indeed, my own convictions. If the use of the means of mass destruction is sin, then the *possession* of the means of mass destruction for the purpose of threatening and deterring the enemy cannot be justified as Christian. Because this threat is effective only if one is also ready to use the weapons, the threat itself is immoral and must also be viewed as *sin*.

The modern military means of mass destruction have changed war so much that the real nature of war is revealed now before everyone's eyes. We have reached the point, therefore, where we must go back and say that all war is irresponsible, is sin, and there can be no justification of it. Every martial threat and positioning which includes the possibility of escalation to universal nuclear war is irresponsible. The current "peace through mutual deterrence" is also irresponsible.

The planned *spiraling of nuclear armaments* threatens us all as never before. We therefore demand immediate and binding arms talks among the great powers. We advocate a European disarmament conference with the declared goal of establishing a zone free from the means of mass destruction. We support a gradual disarmament in the area of conventional arms and the agreed upon building up of cooperation in Europe and Asia, in particular in areas of economic justice.

The service of peace then must become the content of life in the community of Jesus Christ. Church institutions and organizations can do no other than encourage and help in the formation of this service of peace among Christians. Service of peace which is alive in the congregation and which is being supported by the church leadership should have these three emphases in mind:

1. *Learning the love of the enemy.* Wars are spread through *friend-foe thinking.* Through artificially concocted images of the enemy, fears are used and aggressions called forth. Through psychological

warfare human beings are led to the disregard for life and mobilized for killings. The command of the love of the enemy enables the dissolution of these images of the enemy and the fears and aggressions which are engendered through them.

If *anxiety before the enemy* is made the counsel of politics, not only external but also internal peace is imperiled. The loyalty of the citizens to the government which has been elected by them is then no longer won through fulfilling the mandate to govern but forced through the spreading of fear, be it fear of enemies of the state, or be it the fear to be considered as an enemy of the state. The spreading of psychological unrest and public mistrust are the results. Whoever wants, on the contrary, to spread peace will resist the use and engendering of fear in our people. Sober historical and political analyses can also free us in Germany from the *fear of Russia,* the *horror of the communists,* and make us capable of the necessary concrete political encounter (as I once answered one who pressed me about the Russian communist threat: "in Moscow also they cook only with water;" he was completely baffled!).

2. *Recognizing the real danger and cooperating on overcoming it.* While taking up again and intensifying this *East-West conflict,* the great powers have repressed from the public awareness the much more dangerous *North-South conflict* and the danger of the *ecological catastrophe.* The politics of the new armament functions at the expense of help for the Third World and leads to its further exploitation. The poor are already today paying for the arming of the rich. Already today time, intelligence and capital are being wasted for instruments of mass destruction and not spent for overcoming hunger in the world. The *Christian's service of peace* in such a situation must also become the voice and advocate of the silent and dying peoples in the midst of the conflict over spiraling armaments.

3. *Becoming a peace church.* The more the church moves from being *a church bound to the state* to a *free church,* the clearer can become its witness to peace and the less ambiguous its initiative for peace. We believe that the church of Jesus Christ can become a church

of peace without sectarian isolation from the world. It will become a peace church to the degree that it confesses *Christ* and Christ alone as its Lord and the peace of the whole world and shows the necessary consequences of this confession.

Two final remarks: I believe that so-called pacifism is no longer an illusion or utopia; pacifism is the only *realism* of life left to us in this apocalyptic situation of threatening world annihilation. Pacifists are the realists of life, and not merely voices of utopia. Second, having come through two world wars with much misery and tragedy, we Christians in Germany do not want to become guilty of a third and last world war. Please understand us and help us make your witness of peace and our witness of peace an emerging common witness of peace.

Part II

In Dialogue with Moltmann

5

Moltmann's Theology of
The Cross

Thomas N. Finger

Jürgen Moltmann's theology of the cross has much in common with the
Anabaptist perspective. For both, the significance of the cross must extend
beyond the sphere of individual salvation. For both, taking up the cross
cannot consist entirely in bearing personal sorrows or crucifying harmful
inner desires. As John Howard Yoder has insisted, to "take up the cross"
means to take up the approach towards life that led Jesus to the cross. It
entails adopting at least a general socio-political orientation. It involves
identifying with oppressed people, rejecting violence, and going counter
to those Powers That Be who live by violence. In short, taking the cross
seriously involves making an at least implicit critique of many systems
and structures of modern life, and thereby risking disfavor, danger, and
even death.

In all these ways, Moltmann is very much in line with traditional
Anabaptism. In one important way, however, his approach is very different.
It is a distinctly theological one. However much his conclusions and even
aspects of his method may differ from those of the systematic theological

73

tradition, he is continually in dialogue with it, and continually contributing to it.

On the other hand, it is commonly supposed that the Anabaptist tradition has very little to say on the more speculative theological themes. Anabaptists—so the common impression runs—have much to say about ethics, discipleship and practical Christian living, but really nothing at all about "speculative" theological topics like soteriology, Christology or the Trinity.

Notice, for instance, some representative quotations from Robert Friedmann's helpful *Theology of Anabaptism*. Of soteriology, which is "traditionally the very nucleus of all theology," Friedmann insists that it "is and cannot be a major theme in Anabaptist thought . . . These early Anabaptists . . . desired to walk in the footsteps of the Master 'in love and cross' . . . Therefore the question of salvation naturally dropped into the background and was dealt with only casually."[1]

Or take Christology. "Turning to the doctrine of the nature of Christ," Friedmann writes, "we again find among the Anabaptists no interest in such speculation." Friedmann does concede that traditional formulations (such as the Chalcedonian Creed) were accepted unreservedly by Anabaptists. "But one feels," Friedmann continues, "that this is not the center, not the decisive element . . . What truly mattered was both the model of the life of Christ and the fact of His death on the cross . . . All speculative, basically 'hellenic' sophistication of patristic theology is left behind."[2]

Or finally, consider the doctrine of the Trinity. As in Christology, Anabaptists affirmed the traditional trinitarian teaching. However, Friedmann insists, "Such an affirmation was not central within their existential approach, and in their own group they hardly ever referred to it." Rather, they accepted it "without hesitation, since it did not in any way interfere with their own particular concern for discipleship and the building up of the Kingdom."[3]

Now much of the theological tradition certainly has discussed soteriology, Christology and the Trinity in ways that are highly abstract,

---

[1] Robert Friedmann, *Theology of Anabaptism* (Scottdale: Herald, 1973) p. 78.

[2] *Ibid.*, pp. 55–56.

[3] *Ibid.*, p. 53.

unrelated to and sometimes even opposed to discipleship. Yet statements like those just quoted seem to say more. They seem to imply that—in its more "speculative" branches, at least—theology has nothing to do with practical Christianity. They also seem to imply the reverse: that the Anabaptist perspective has nothing significant to contribute to the "speculative" areas of theology.

Friedmann's remarks about the original Anabaptists also apply to many in Mennonite and similar circles today. Many are constantly stressing peace, social justice and community. But if one should ask what all this has to do with salvation, or with God—one often receives an embarrassed grin, a few inarticulate groans . . . and perhaps a lot more on peace and justice and community.

This need not mean that such persons have no theological beliefs. Not a few frequently express orthodox convictions through song and hear them from the pulpit. Here again the comparison with early Anabaptism is apt. It's not that either group necessarily rejects the basic "speculative" affirmations of Christendom. It's more that neither group can see any important connection—or at least, can articulate any important connection—between these beliefs and what seems to matter most in concrete Christian living.

But is it the case that reflection on more "speculative" theological themes has little to do with discipleship? And is it the case that the Anabaptist orientation has nothing to contribute to scholarly discussion on these themes? I have chosen to discuss Moltmann's theology of the cross partly because Moltmann presents a powerful case that the way of the cross, which he affirms most profoundly, can best be traversed when one grasps its theological significance. I have also chosen this theme because it provides an intriguing example of how one who shares many Anabaptist convictions goes to work within the theological tradition.

The Cross and Soteriology

How is the cross related to Salvation? If "the cross" functions largely as a catch-word for a kind of lifestyle or a code of ethics, one would suppose that salvation is attained largely by acting in accordance with it. If we do our best, one might think, we will somehow participate in salvation. But if our understanding of soteriology stops here, we can come perilously close to the works-righteousness so heavily critiqued in the New Testament.

Jürgen Moltmann's soteriology is deeply influenced by Martin Luther's "Theses" for the Heidelberg Disputation of 1518. Among Mennonites, of course, Luther is in some disrepute. Was he not, after all, the archetypal Protestant who so sharply split the inner, spiritual Kingdom from the outer, political one—and who restricted his revolutionary insights to the former? Moltmann largely agrees with this Anabaptist critique of Luther.[4] Nevertheless, in these early theses, which predate Luther's developed thinking on the "two kingdoms," Moltmann finds insights capable of transforming soteriology in both its personal and social dimensions.[5]

Following Luther, Moltmann starts not from the standpoint of practical Christianity, but from the more "speculative" theological questions: how do we know about God? What is God like? He begins by contrasting two ways of understanding God's nature. The first is philosophical. It begins by reflecting on observable phenomena and reasoning "upwards" towards God as their ultimate Source or Cause. For instance, in our world one finds things, people or events characterized by some degree of power, some kind of beauty, or some sort of wisdom. One then infers from these that their ultimate Source must be supremely Powerful, Beautiful and Wise. (This is the *via eminentiae* popular in Medieval theology: for instance, in Thomas Aquinas' fourth "way.")

Now Moltmann doesn't argue that this philosophical approach is entirely incorrect. But he insists (like Luther) that it usually leads us to act in the wrong way. For if we suppose that God is supremely Powerful, Beautiful and Wise, then we normally assume that to be like God we must acquire more power, attain more wisdom, and become more beautiful. And so we set out to gain more of these things—to become more Godlike and to please God—through our own efforts.

The second approach to understanding God, however, does not survey the world at large and search for clues to God's character. It begins with God's self-revelation. How do we know what God is like? According to this second way, by looking at Jesus—and especially Jesus on the cross.

---

[4] Jürgen Moltmann, *The Crucified God* (New York: Harper, 1974) pp. 72–73.
[5] For what follows, *ibid.*, pp. 68–73, 207–219. The biblical text to which Moltmann most frequently refers is 1 Corinthians 1:18ff.

And if we look at the cross, what kind of God do we see? One who is obviously and overwhelmingly powerful, wise and beautiful? No. We see a God encompassed by weakness, a God apparently ensnared in the most senseless foolishness, a God marred by repulsive ugliness.

This second approach to understanding God (by looking "downwards," as it were, rather than "upwards") also has implications for our actions. If God is revealed amidst that which the world regards as weak, stupid and ugly, then we must take a new look at these things. Maybe if we take more seriously those who are weak and suffer, those situations fraught with senseless tragedy, riddled with ugly brokenness— maybe there we will find God. And maybe we will become less enamored with the human striving for power, wisdom and beauty. For this striving, after all, has produced many victims and has spawned much of the suffering, tragedy and brokenness in this world.

If we press this line of thinking further, the cross yields principles of social criticism. It provides a standpoint from which to critique systems of power and wealth, and from which to initiate remedies for social disenfranchisement and poverty. Mennonites have discerned many such implications, even if they may not have thought of them in just this way.

But the cross, so understood, also has profound soteriological meaning on the personal level. For if I take God's cruciform revelation seriously, I must acknowledge that deep down I too long to be powerful, wise and beautiful. I must admit that I too am terribly afraid of being weak and stupid and ugly. I am afraid of failure. I am afraid of dying. But, Moltmann continues, if I keep my gaze on the cross, I begin to realize that God himself became weak, foolish and ugly. God himself entered into the pain and horror of failure. God even entered into death. And yet God was not finally conquered by these.

Now if I fully grasp this, says Moltmann, I become ashamed of my fearful longing and striving for power, wisdom and beauty. For it was these strivings, in the person of Jesus' religious and political enemies, that put him to death. And I am brought to repentance.

Repentance, however, is not some heroic introspective effort to strangle these strivings in oneself, not some mighty moral resolve to wholly redirect one's actions. True repentance is possible only when we realize—perhaps just implicitly—that if Christ went through weakness, failure and death, and that these did not destroy him . . . then if we abandon our fearful attempts to establish our own strength, success and our very existence, we too will not be destroyed.

The essential soteriological meaning of the cross, then, is that God himself experienced suffering and death, and was not destroyed; consequently, if we go through these things in union with him, we too will not be destroyed. We will not be abandoned. Nothing can ever separate us from the love of God in Christ Jesus.

When and insofar as I truly apprehend this (or better: insofar as I am apprehended by this God), then I can begin taking up my own cross. In union with Jesus, I can begin crucifying my own inner fears and strivings. And I can take my place in opposition to such strivings as they manifest themselves in society. For the critique of the cross, as we said, also carried powerful soteriological meaning for society.

Accordingly, approaching the cross from the standpoint of soteriology as Moltmann does will not diminish its significance for ethics or discipleship. On the contrary, it strengthens it. For we cannot effectively critique and reform the strivings for power, wisdom and beauty which corrupt society if we are still enslaved to them. If the crucified God is not enabling us to crucify their roots in ourselves, whatever we do will ultimately spring from them, and perpetuate their influence—perhaps in a much subtler form. On the other hand, the more assured we are of the presence of the crucified One, the more authentically will we be able to withstand the social opposition of these forces, and to suffer it, as Jesus did, in genuine love.

The Cross and Christology

Moltmann's book, *The Crucified God*, from which most of this material comes, is much less concerned with soteriology than with Christology and the Trinity. Moltmann, in fact, insists that we cannot really know what the cross means for us until we grasp what it means for God. In this volume, theology is not primarily reflection on ethics or experience, from which one seeks to derive some understanding of God. It is instead an effort to ground all ethics and self-understanding in the doctrine of God.

Many, of course (and not only Anabaptists), would object that Christology leads into the most abstruse speculations. What possible relevance could discussion about natures, persons and essences in the Godhead have for discipleship? Moltmann, however, does not begin with such concepts. He begins with the history of God's activity, focusing particularly on the event we have just discussed: the cross. Let us reflect more deeply on what we just said about it.[6]

What lies at the core of the soteriological significance of the cross? It is the conviction—unarticulated though it may have been—that God himself experienced suffering and death . . . and that therefore God is with one in these things. But examined more closely, such a conviction implies that this Jesus who suffered and died and is with one is not merely a moral example—though of course he is that. It implies that he is not merely a social critic—though of course he is that. Beyond these, it also implies that somehow this Jesus is . . . God. Or at least that God is present in Jesus: so deeply, in fact, that when Jesus suffers, dies and rises, all this happens in God . . . and *this* is why the cross has saving significance.

Now all of this, of course, may be extremely unclear conceptually. A Christological conviction about the Deity of Jesus is not normally something that one first grasps intellectually, and for which one later finds ethical or experiential applications. Usually it is something that one first grasps implicitly, and that demands conceptual clarification as one probes its meaning more deeply. For Moltmann, Christological (and Trinitarian) affirmations are not intellectual speculations. Rather, formulating and affirming them become necessary as one seeks to grasp the historical and soteriological reality of the Christian faith in depth.

Let us look more closely, then, at Jesus' history.[7] Throughout his ministry, Jesus is in closest communion with the One he calls "Father." He teaches about his Father, prays to his Father, obeys his Father. His "Father" is clearly God. However, this identity of purpose is so close that Jesus himself exercises functions appropriate only to God. The coming of God's Kingdom coincides with the coming of Jesus. He speaks with authority appropriate only to God. He forgives sins as only God can. In

---

[6] In the following two paragraphs, we are not yet showing how Moltmann develops his Christology historically. Instead, to give continuity to our exposition, we are indicating how Moltmann's developed Christology is related to what we just said about his appropriation of Luther's "theology of the cross." We do not mean to imply that Moltmann derives his Christology primarily from analysis of soteriological awareness.

[7] See esp. *ibid.,* pp. 145–53, 120–25.

79

short, the message and reality of the Kingdom of God are so inextricably bound up with the person of Jesus that he himself can be none other than God in person.

Yet when Jesus dies on the cross, he is shockingly abandoned by God. He cries out in agony: "My God! My God! Why hast thou forsaken me?"

When we ponder this contrast in depth, how strange it appears! We seem to have God crying out to God. We seem to have God being abandoned . . . yet being abandoned by God. Were this event of little importance, we could perhaps push this perplexity aside. But the cross is the very starting-point of our knowledge of God! How, then, shall we seek to apprehend it? Moltmann insists that we cannot do justice to the issues which Christology raises so long as we operate with a simple, self-identical concept of God. To apprehend the cross, we must make some differentiations in what we mean by "God." In other words, Christology leads inevitably to Trinitarian thinking.

The Cross and the Trinity

To many, the Trinity seems the most abstract of all theological subjects, the one most distant from discipleship. But for Moltmann, Trinitarian doctrine, properly understood, arises from efforts to apprehend more significantly the history of God's action in the world, particularly that of the cross. Moltmann calls the cross the "matter" of the Trinity, and the Trinity the "form" of the cross.[8] Let us follow him, then, as he unfolds the doctrine of the Trinity through focusing on different aspects of the cross.

A. *The Meaning of the Cross for the Son.* We will not grasp the deepest significance of the cross from the standpoint of ethics. We cannot even do so from the standpoint of soteriology. Rather, we must ask what it means for God. For Moltmann, Christology merges into trinitarian doctrine as he begins to ask what the cross meant for the Son.

For the Son, the cross was a horrifying experience of abandonment. He had come proclaiming the arrival of God's Kingdom—an arrival which, we have seen, was intrinsically connected with his own. The Son had

---

[8] *Ibid.,* p. 246.

experienced constant unity with his Father. But then in Gethsemane he began to sense that the One Whom he had known so intimately was withdrawing. Jesus was delivered over to those who hated him: he was deserted, mocked, tortured, killed. "Jesus clearly died with every expression of the most profound horror."[9]

To apprehend this horror, we must remember what the cross meant in Jesus' time. It was hardly a religious symbol. It was brutal, torturous execution by a tyrannical government. The one crucified was not only cast out and execrated by civil society; such a person was also regarded as cursed and rejected by God.

Moltmann sharply contrasts the suffering of a martyr devoted to a good cause with suffering which involves total rejection.[10] He finds a great distinction between suffering when, on one hand, one has a sense of inner justification and the support of others, and, on the other, when one experiences the final, overwhelming sense of aloneness and rejection. For Moltmann, Jesus experienced complete aloneness and rejection—even from God. We can think of this experience of utter godforsakenness as Hell.

According to Moltmann, this abandonment belonged uniquely to Jesus' cross. In this way, the cross of Christ is not like the cross you and I bear. For if we take up our cross and suffer, no matter how badly we suffer, we do so in union with Jesus. We do not die alone. But Jesus died alone. To use traditional language, he died in our place, in our stead: he bore for us the curse of abandonment, the curse of rejection.

B. *The Meaning of the Cross for the Father.* If God the Son suffers abandonment by the Father, it might seem as if God the Father bore some attitude of rejection, judgment, or wrath towards the Son. Indeed, Christian piety and Christian theology have often visualized the cross in this way. God the Father, so to speak, is sometimes pictured as situated above the cross, pouring down on the Son the wrath that all sinners deserve.

Yet this way of thinking, rather than drawing us towards God's saving action on the cross, can push us away. For although we may identify with

---

[9] *Ibid.*, p. 146.
[10] *Ibid.*, pp. 55–56, 63–64, 145–46.

the Son in his suffering, the Father seems overwhelmingly angry, and just barely appeased by the suffering of his Son.[11]

Moltman, however, sees the Father also as suffering.[12] He often refers to Romans 8:32: "He who did not spare his own Son, but delivered him up for us all, will he not also give us all things together with him?!" This passage, at least, refers to the grief, the agony of the Father in delivering up the Son. At the cross, then, the Father also suffers—though Father and Son suffer in different ways. The Son, as we said, suffers abandonment. But only the Father, according to Moltmann, suffers death. For, precisely speaking, those who die do not suffer death. When we die we cease to feel. But we suffer only when we can feel. Consequently, only God the Father "suffers death," bearing the grief of seeing a loved one suffer up to and through the final pain of loss.

C. *The Meaning of the Cross for the Spirit.* In *The Crucified God,* despite his repeated use of the term "Trinity," Moltmann says comparatively little about the Holy Spirit (in this respect he reflects the Western theological tradition's tendency to concentrate on the relationship of Father and Son, and to more or less tack on the Spirit at the end). However, in this work he refers to the Spirit as what issues from the interaction between Father and Son on the cross:

> Whatever proceeds from this event . . . must be understood as the spirit of the surrender of the Father and the Son, as the spirit which creates love for forsaken men . . . It is the unconditioned and therefore boundless love which proceeds from the grief of the Father and the dying of the Son and reaches forsaken men in order to create in them the possibility and the force of new life.[13]

---

[11] Despite the inadequacies of this picture (which is my illustration, not Moltmann's, it seems that the New Testament does occasionally speak of Jesus bearing the judgment or wrath of God: 2 Cor 5:21, Gal 3:13, Heb 9:28, 1 John 2:1–2, etc). Moltmann, however, often speaks as if Jesus' Kingdom message replaced the notion of divine judgment with that of divine love *(ibid.,* pp. 128–35). Moltmann espouses a "universalist" position that all human beings are saved by Christ's work.

[12] *Ibid.,* pp. 242–43.

[13] *Ibid.,* p. 245.

However, Moltmann's recent book, *The Trinity and the Kingdom,* says much more about the Spirit.[14] Moltmann goes back through Jesus' life and notices that he is baptized by the Spirit, driven into the wilderness by the Spirit, and performs mighty acts through the Spirit. Moltmann also emphasizes those many New Testament passages which talk about the Son being raised through the Spirit, and about the Spirit baptizing people into the Father and Son, or into the life of God. This broader treatment shows that his trinitarian theology is not focused narrowly on the cross, but on the overarching historical sweep from creation to consummation.

D. *The Meaning of the Cross for the Divine Nature.* What is at the core of the Oneness of the Father, Son and Spirit? What do they share that makes them divine? Moltmann says little about a divine "nature" or "essence." His main point is that the persons of the Trinity are united in purpose, in will. Even in their most painful separation from one another, even in their deepest agony on the cross, Father and Son remain united in purpose. Thus, while Moltmann does mention a unity of divine "substance," he seems to define this "substance" almost entirely in terms of this unity of will.[15]

Moltmann departs from traditional discussions of the divine "nature" in at least one other respect.[16] According to the theological tradition, God is "eternal"; hence, God cannot die. Understandably, the tradition encountered difficulties when it considered Jesus' death. For he was fully divine . . . and yet he died. Theologians usually solved this by saying that, strictly speaking, it was only Jesus' "human nature" which suffered and died. Of course, that human nature was so closely intertwined with his "divine nature" that the latter was brought into very close connection with death. But few traditional theologians went so far as to say that Christ's divine nature, or that God, actually died.

Yet this is precisely what Moltmann means to say. It is the fact that God went through death which gives us confidence in God's presence

---

[14] *The Trinity and the Kingdom* (New York: Harper, 1981) pp. 65–94. In another of Moltmann's major theological works, *The Church in the Power of the Spirit* (New York: Harper, 1977), the Spirit plays a major role.

[15] *The Crucified God,* p. 244.

[16] *Ibid.,* pp. 227–35.

when we go through it too. Think again of his picture of the cross. Down below, as it were, is the Son abandoned by the Father. Up above, so to speak, is the Father grieving over the death of the Son, yet allowing the Son to be abandoned. Moltmann says that this grief and pain which stretches apart the Deity becomes wide enough, as it were, for the whole world to fit within it.

In other words, when God enters into the pain and suffering of death, when God experiences abandonment and grief in their most powerful form, God identifies with all the sufferings which ever occurred. This means that all of humankind is taken up into the infinite love of God:

> Only if all disaster, forsakenness by God, absolute death, the infinite curse of damnation and sinking into nothingness is in God himself, is community with this God eternal salvation, infinite joy, indestructible election and divine life. The bifurcation in God must contain the whole uproar of history within itself.[17]

On the cross, God opened himself to grief and abandonment. And as God opened himself, this made room for anyone else who suffers to enter and to experience not only sympathy, but the actual presence of God—a presence which ultimately extends beyond suffering and creates new hope and life. Or, to use another of Moltmann's images, the Trinity is "open." Theological tradition has often pictured the Trinity as a kind of "closed circle" in heaven. But for Moltmann, the Trinity has always been open for people on earth: God has always been seeking fellowship with humans and seeking to share their experiences. And by actually dying, God has opened himself in the widest possible sense.[18]

E. *The Meaning of the Cross for the Divine Attributes.* The theological tradition has extensively discussed the so-called "attributes" of God: immutability, omnipotence, eternity, etc. Moltmann's general relationship to this tradition is well exemplified in the way he treats them. On one hand, he feels this discussion is meaningful and devotes some space to it. On the other, his own views often depart sharply from the common ones.

---

[17] *Ibid.*, p. 246.
[18] *Ibid.*, p. 249.

He is attempting, in other words, to introduce some very different considerations into the theological tradition itself.

Theologians have sometimes talked about divine "immutability" in such a way that God seems static and wholly untouched by change of any sort. Clearly, if Moltmann is to find any use for this term, he cannot define it in this way. For if God died on the cross, God experienced something new. God changed. Moltmann, however, finds it still meaningful to affirm that God's essential character never changes. He finds it significant to assert that God's fundamental purposes never change. On the cross we observe a consistency of character and purpose despite the most profound opposition and pain. In this sense theology can and should speak of God as "immutable."[19]

Some Implications of the Cross

Throughout this article I have been not only explaining Moltmann's theology of the cross, but also indicating its relevance for discipleship as Anabaptists see it. In closing, let me make this relevance more concrete by indicating several implications.

A. *Community.* Moltmann's understanding of the Trinity provides the strongest possible theological foundation for the Anabaptist emphasis on community. Moltmann is saying that God is essentially a community of persons. God is not just a vague, mysterious force. Neither is God a single, isolated, self-sufficient person. God is essentially an intertwining of relationships marked by self-giving, response, acknowledgment, sharing, and enjoyment of one another.

This is the deepest reason why true salvation cannot be individualistic. For to participate in the Life of God is to enter into this process of giving and sharing. To truly enter it involves being drawn into closer relationships with others.

When Mennonites try to explain to our individualistic culture why Christian living involves community, they sometimes simply insist that Jesus commanded it. This is true enough. But this answer leaves us with

---

[19] *Ibid.*, p. 229.

Jesus as an isolated, commanding individual set over against his community. We fail to see Jesus himself as one who walked in continuous obedience and love towards his Father and experienced the continuous presence of the Spirit. And we fail to see that Christ's community not only follows him, but is also caught up into his life which he shares with his Father and his Spirit.

B. *Society and the Church.* So long as people think of God as a single being existing "above" us and apart from us, they may well assume that society should be structured in hierarchical fashion. If God is a single ruler who gives commands, then we ought to have a single political authority who makes the rules and enforces them. And we also ought to have churches in which a single pastor calls the shots and runs the show.

But if God is trinitarian, and if salvation involves participation in this trinitarian Life, then God's relationship to humanity will be less one of command and obedience, and more one of sharing, working together and mutual interaction. This would imply that social structures should be not hierarchical, but mutual, reciprocal and open to the participation of as many as possible. And our churches should encourage corporate decision-making and leadership.[20]

C. *Feminism.* All along, of course, I have been using the terms "Father" and "Son." To many, such terms connote a masculine view of God. I have employed them, however, not only because they reflect Moltmann's usage, but also because I believe, as he does, that their biblical use conveys not patriarchy but intimacy. By customarily calling God "Father," Jesus revealed the personal, compassionate side of Yahweh more fully than did the Old Testament. And he also revealed the tender, mutually loving relationship of Father and Son.

In other words, the deepest significance of "Father" and "Son" is to express characteristics that we often think of as more "feminine" than "masculine." And feminine imagery seems even more appropriate for other features of Moltmann's Trinity. He speaks of the whole world, with all its grief and pain, being caught up by and carried within the love of God. Rather than speaking of God as carrying the world within "himself," might we not more appropriately talk of God carrying the world within "herself,"

---

[20] See *The Trinity and the Kingdom*, pp. 191–202.

as a mother carried a child?[21] Does not Moltmann's major emphasis on the passion and compassion of God correspond more closely with what we more often associate with women than with men?

D. *Anabaptism and Theology.* Hopefully, this article has stimulated questions as to whether contemporary Anabaptists might not profit from more serious involvement in theology. We have seen how Moltmann considers the cross not only from the standpoint of ethics and discipleship, but from that of soteriology. I have argued that such an approach is hardly irrelevant to ethical and social concerns, but complements and undergirds them. We have also seen how Moltmann seeks to ground all this in the doctrine of God. By so doing, he has provided deep foundations for concerns such as community, social and ecclesiastical reform, and feminism.

Perhaps Moltmann's deepest reason for pursuing these topics theologically might be stated as follows. When we examine in depth the tasks to which we are called, the joys and hopes which are to motivate us, and the suffering and grief which we are to endure, we discover that we are called not to perform merely human tasks with some help from God. We find, instead, that all such joys and sufferings have already been experienced and taken up into the life of God. If we know that God has experienced all the glorious hope of the inbreaking Kingdom, and all the inexpressible anguish of failure and death, we know that we are never alone, no matter what may happen. We know that our aspirations and our struggles are grounded in the fundamental movement of the universe.

Finally, we have also seen how one with convictions close to those of Anabaptists has had great impact on the theological tradition. Moltmann belongs within the tradition in the sense that he finds most of its major questions significant and works by recognized scholarly methods. But he is quite different from the tradition in the way that he answers many of these questions. Notions such as God dying, or the Trinity as the "form" of the cross—these are relatively novel. Nevertheless, they have sparked much serious attention and won much acceptance. This indicates that the theological tradition is very open to the type of insights found in the Anabaptist tradition. The time is ripe for articulating other Anabaptist insights in theological fashion.

---

[21] *Ibid.*, pp. 108–11

6

Response to Moltmann's "The Lutheran Doctrine of the Two Kingdoms and Its Use Today"

Clarence Bauman

At this stage my function perhaps should be to recapitulate a very complex situation in a few simple premises so that we can get along with our dialogue.

I would like to make some indications and reservations "*kurz und spitz*," i.e., quite to the point and concisely. I will state first of all Luther's position as elementally as I possibly can in a descriptive way and then move on to his intrinsic self-understanding, his *Selbstverständnis*, his rationale for that position and its theological self-justification. And thirdly, I will indicate my own reservations in terms of evaluations and implications of Luther's position.

Jesus taught: "resist not evil with evil" (Matt 5:39—note dative of means). Paul advised: "overcome evil with good" (also dative of means—Rom 12:21). Since the Roman Catholic church couldn't 'rhyme' these texts with life—as Luther said—i.e., with the sword, therefore they taught: *"Christus habe solchs nicht gepotten, sondern den Volkomenen geratten."* (WA 11, 245, 18f.). That is, Christ did not command the Sermon on the Mount, but he gave it to us as counsel for the 'perfect' ones (*consilia* for the *status perfectionis*), i.e., for the monks, for the clergy. Despite the separation of clergy and laity, however, both realms were confused, Luther thought, for the Pope in the crusades against the Turks waged holy rather than merely secular war. That's the problem.

To set the record straight and presumably solve the problem, Luther declared that God rules the world in two ways: through law and gospel (*Gesetz und Evangelium*). And that constitutes what is known as the order of maintenance and the order of redemption (*Erhaltungsordnung und Erlösungsordnung*). Law holds the world together, love moves it forward. This constitutes then two contrasting modes of rule (*Herrschaftsweisen*) and these may never be mixed or confused. Luther said very explicitly: *"Ein Fürst kann wohl ein Christ sein"* (WA 32, 440). A prince can be a Christian and vice versa, so long as it remains perfectly clear that his secular vocation has nothing in common with his Christian profession.

The person is indeed a Christian, but his office, his vocation, has nothing to do with his being a Christian. In the secular office or *Amt* it doesn't belong (or fit) how you are to suffer for Christ and how you are to act for Christ. That remains all for your "Christ-person" (*"da gehöret nicht her wie du gegen Gott leben . . . tun und leiden sollst, das las für deine Christperson gehen,"* ibid.).

Since the secular *Amt* is ordained of God, Luther held that the hand that wields the sword is no longer *Menschen Hand, sondern Gottes Hand* (not man's hand, but God's hand). *"Und nicht der Mensch, sondern Gott hängt, rädert, enthauptet, würgt, und kriegt"* ("Not man, but God, hangs, racks on the wheel, decapitates [executes] strangles, and wars"). *"Nicht ich schlage, stosse, and tote, sondern Gott und mein Fürst, dessen Diener meine Hand und mein Leben sind"* ("Not I slay, stab and kill, but God and my prince whose servant my hand and my life is" [*Ob Kriegsleute auch in seligen Stand sein können*, WA 19, 626]).

So life demands both the clenched fist and the outstretched arm of Jesus (*"die gepanzerte Faust and die Hand Jesu"*), as Naumann well said. The main thing is not to seek to rule society by the Sermon on the Mount, and that has been emphasized over and over again by theologians like

Niebuhr and Nygren and many others; that's '*schwarmerish*,' idealistic fanaticism, instead of what is required, namely, pragmatic secular realism. In other words Luther might well say: When I stand up in the pulpit and someone attacks me for the sake of the Gospel, then I suffer as a faithful servant of Jesus Christ. But when someone attacks me for the sake of the prince's land then I hold my dagger upon his head. So an Anabaptist asks Luther: some night you are riding through a dark forest, the *Schwarzwald*, and someone attacks you right suddenly—will you have time to ask if it's for the *Evangelium*, for the Gospel's sake, or for the land? Doesn't Luther's *Zwei-Reiche-Lehre* (two-kingdom-teaching) imply, as Professor Moltmann ably developed, the schizophrenic dichotomy of the person? Doesn't it undermine the integrity and the unity of the Christian self? To this existential dilemma Luther responded variously:

1. Each person on earth has two persons: a "Christ-person" in which respect he is bound solely to God and a "Welt-person" in which he is bound to others. The moral effect of this distinction is Luther's insistence, that one's entire Christian being remains entirely invisible. The Christian as a Christian expresses nothing that can be discerned as having a Christ nature in the outer life; the manner of the outer life belongs to the secular realm. In other words, the entire Christian being remains entirely invisible so that *Nachfolge Christi* within the church invisible is reduced to a pure spiritualism (except for the Word and Sacrament).

2. As a "Christ-person" one remains *simul iustus et peccator*—simultaneously justified and sinful, according to Romans 7—and this two-fold designation binds one both *ontologically*, in terms of one's original sin (*Erbsünde*), and *morally*, in the sense of *duty*, to the order for the world (*Weltordnung*).

3. Luther claimed that true Christians belong to God's kingdom and that they need neither worldly sword nor law *for themselves*, but only for their sick neighbors. But Luther was unable to say *who* these true Christians really were or how one might identify them, if not by their deeds or character since on principle they must remain anonymous within the *ecclesia invisibilis*.

4. In contrast to pagans and fanatics, Luther held that Christians must rule and wield the sword *in love*. As judge, hangman, or

soldier they must dutifully perform their *act,* but withhold any evil intention. In Lutheran ethics this casuistry is known as *Gesinnungslehre* (ethical intention), and is exemplified by the soul-stirring prayer of an American Lutheran chaplain who on August 5, 1945, blessed the Hiroshima H-bomb mission—so as to withhold any evil intention.

Finally, Luther's two-kingdom-teaching has been described as an *Irrgarten,* a maize of unsolved logical and moral contradictions. I cite only four.

If God and his will are one, which seems to me to be the elemental presupposition of all theological reflection, whether Christian or Jewish, why claim that secular authorities are subject only to God, but not to his will as revealed in Christ's teaching?

Second, if Christ's teaching is excluded on principle from all secular office, by what criterion of discernment is one to distinguish that administration from the power of the devil—from evil itself?

Third, when will intelligent theologians begin to understand that the Sermon on the Mount is Jesus' interpretation of exactly how God's law is to be lived in this world here and now by all who profess His name—that Jesus' *Berglehre* is not some impractical hypothetical irrelevance to be spiritualized in some other cloud-world kookoo-land where there are no enemies to love, as if what Jesus said applied to a different time than *now* or in a different way than then? As though Jesus didn't say what he meant or didn't mean what he said!

Finally, who in the final analysis determines what constitutes my responsibility? Jesus? Or the draft board?

7

Response to Moltmann's "Barth's Doctrine of the Lordship of Christ and the Experience of the Confessing Church"

John Howard Yoder

I'd like to record, without wanting to pursue them, two quibbles about reading church history before taking up the issue more central to the dialogue.

Yesterday one of the students asked a question about the fallen world. Professor Moltmann said he's not sure that the world should be spoken of as fallen. Today he referred to Barth's use of Romans 13 and the particular understanding of "powers" that Barth had borrowed from Cullmann as odd. I doubt that that is an adequate way to deal with the set of New Testament texts, in which the language of "principalities and powers" still seems to me to have more to say than Moltmann grants. If we take all of the Pauline language of "powers" together (of course that's an exegetical assumption, namely, that we should read all of those passages in relation to each other), one must say at the same time three things: that the powers are good creations, and fallen, and coming under the lordship of Christ. That complexity would seem to me to promise more adequacy in solving this problem of where the line runs than if we were to say that people are fallen but the world isn't. It seems rather that the *exousiology* of Paul does talk about other levels of fallenness, other locations of fallenness, to which the ministry of Christ as Lamb and Lord also has relevance. But that would mean going into Paul.

The other point, also about Paul, would be whether to follow the division introduced by some scholars between *Corinthians,* which is Paul proper, and Ephesians and Colossians, which represent an undesirable or regrettable enthusiastic development out of Paul, and not Paul himself. There would be reason to discuss that, and it would make a difference, but I would rather not concentrate on that; I just take note that it is a question.

I would like to take up a more central issue, one mentioned earlier. How do we assess the experience of the Confessing Church—e.g., Barth's counsel to people to stay in the state church—and its gradual assimilation into the state church structure after the war. This is not just a historical challenge. It has to do with the theology behind the history that happened and the history that didn't happen.

The Confessing Church story is a remarkable story of theology producing action, clear thinking resulting in structural change. But it is also a story of that action not growing in clarity with time, but rather becoming more and more diffuse. The real victory of the Confessing Church was not that it kept doing its thing with great clarity; it was rather a number of people catching on to a number of proper insights through the 1930s and into the 40s. Then it was ratified by the fact that the outside world—first the ecumenical world, and then the occupying forces reorganizing Germany—recognized the leaders of the Confessing Church as the leaders of the post-war German established Evangelical church.

How did it happen that the leaders of the Confessing Church, practically all in jail when the war ended and whom the allies then helped become the bishops and presidents of the land churches, accepted stepping back into an established church situation instead of going on being a free church. I once had the occasion in 1955 to ask Martin Niemoller that.

He said in effect, "We're sorry, we shouldn't have." The desire not to make a schism, not to step out until you're pushed out, stood in tension with the language of the gathered church which was already present in Confessing Church thought more than people realized at the time. People didn't realize, at the time Barth wrote his pamphlet on *The Christian Community and the Citizen Community*, that this was the first time for centuries in mainline Protestant theology in Europe that somebody had conceived of the society at large as not being coterminous with the believing community. That was a profound insight, which Barth knew was dictated by his theology, but he hadn't spelled out how radical it was. As a result, it wasn't as radical as it might have been. People could keep talking that way and going on with the state church structure, with its linkage with the economy and the rest of society, as that was preserved by the allied occupying forces, because they thought it would help to keep the country together. *The Gathered Congregation* was the title of a little booklet by Professor Otto Weber, Professor Moltmann's teacher, which Harold Bender showed me with a smile in 1949, saying, "Here is somebody from a good university faculty talking about a believers' church, unfolding a vision of the church which would not depend upon the state, which would be made up of people who affirm that they believe, and would be structured from that confession."

The difficulty with the Confessing Church is that it didn't find ways permanently to incarnate the theological insight that the way for Christ's lordship to be proclaimed in the wider society is to have a visible body carrying it instead of having that proclamation contradicted by a secretive church, a non-democratic church, a church without free speech, a church without equality, etc.

So the question I am looking at is illustrated by the history, but it is not a historical question. What is the potential of this theology, if properly understood, especially with the wisdom of hindsight, to guide in producing the kind of empirical church that could be an appropriate vehicle for that kind of message of Christ's lordship? Barth didn't get his theological insight from the empirical church. He got it from rethinking the roots of ecclesiology from a biblical Christology. Barth called for a different kind of church; he never saw it come into being. Should he have?

8

Response to Moltmann's "Political Theology and Political Hermeneutics"

Helmut Harder

In his discussion of what it means to follow Jesus Christ in the world today, Jürgen Moltmann presents, in his third lecture, a lucid description of current political theology. His apparent purpose is not to assess this theological movement, but to show how it offers a better option for understanding our Christian responsibility than we have in the scheme suggested by Luther or Barth. From this standpoint Moltmann's presentation of political theology is stimulating and informative. However, it is necessary for the sake of the quest for a valid framework for Christian responsibility to also look critically at the political theology which Moltmann commends. Does the critical hermeneutics as outlined by Moltmann remain faithful to the "true Christ" (p. 38)? The comments that follow will speak to this question by highlighting one questionable aspect of what is otherwise an appealing framework for theological reconstruction.

Moltmann begins by observing that for the new political theology "*praxis* becomes the criterion of truth" (p. 35). It follows that one must take a critical attitude toward reality, and especially toward political existence and social functions. The function of criticism is to open up new possibilities for the future of humanity. In this connection eschatology becomes both the foundation and the medium of one's theological outlook and passion. That is, one's history and one's present life must be awakened, grasped, and changed by a zeal which is fed by the eschatological vision of the coming kingdom of God.

Crucial to Moltmann's view is the Christological basis which he provides for the contemporary implications of Jesus' messianic message. He begins with the defensible statement that "Jesus' messianic message and deeds may be summarized by the concept of *eschatological anticipation*" (p. 39). The implication that follows is that the followers of Jesus in the world today are led forward toward the messianic future by the power of anticipation engendered by Jesus.

Having established the relation of Christology to eschatology, Moltmann proceeds to make a point which is questionable. He states: "But if Jesus is the *anticipator* of God then he must simultaneously and unavoidably become the sign of opposition to the powers of a world which is opposed to God and to this world's laws which are closed to the future" (p. 39). It is at this point that our question arises. How does the view of Jesus as "anticipator of God" establish the basis for "opposition to the powers of a world which is opposed to God?" Moltmann provides us with no theological basis for this connection. He simply states that the followers of Christ are inspired by "the practical passion to renew life now in the spirit of the resurrection" (p. 40).

But inspiration and passion for renewal do not provide a trustworthy basis for Christian ethics. Nor does the wrongness of the world or the proneness of the church to follow traditional ways or the status quo of political rule. Yet these are suggested by Moltmann as the motivation and legitimation for the way of Jesus' followers. One may have expected that an appeal would be made to the power of love as a final touchstone for ethics. But in the end even love is relativized or possibly set aside. In the struggle for the achievement of justice, says Moltmann, "love remains fragmentary" (p. 46).

We find that Moltmann's understanding of Christology takes the *message* of Jesus regarding the kingdom of God seriously, but does not take Jesus' *method* of action into account with equal care. Indeed the *way* of Jesus does not provide, in Moltmann's description of political theology, the basis for the way of Jesus' disciples.

It is at this point that the question must be raised as to whether political theology is based on the "true Christ." Moltmann wants this to be the case. He says: "Not christology nor messianism as such, but *Jesus* makes the messianism of the political theology we here describe specifically *Christian*" (p. 38). But one can argue that in his way of putting the matter the determining norm for Christian ethics is not the way of Jesus Christ but rather a messianic vision which is impassioned by a zeal for the messianic kingdom of God rather than by the way of Jesus. And we are left to our own ethical decisions when it comes to choosing the means of achieving the end. What matters above all else is that we enter the struggle against exploitation, oppression, alienation, destruction and apathy in the firm conviction that although death may be our lot, the resurrection will vindicate our cause. There is always the related comfort that it is impossible in any case to keep one's hands clean and one's heart altogether pure. In the meantime it is possible to celebrate that which we anticipate.

It is true, as Moltmann states, that Christian theology "must grasp (Jesus) and his history in an eschatological way" (p. 38). However in doing so, Christian theology must take care that it does not transgress an essential element in the way of Jesus as established by him and his history: the way of non-violence. Unfortunately Moltmann's attempt to build a bridge between Jesus Christ and our situation loses sight of Jesus' call to non-violence. It is not that Jesus' situation was different from the plight of those who suffer injustice in our time. Surely he could have legitimated the move to violence—as is done in political theology—on the basis that the acts of the oppressor give ample cause for a "just war" of liberation. But Jesus renounced any violent campaign against the oppressor. His mandate is clear: "Do not resist one who is evil. But if any one strikes you on the right cheek, turn to him the other also" (Matt 5:39). Or, "put your sword back into its place, for all who take the sword will perish by the sword" (Matt 26:52). Here we find no ambiguity regarding the process of life that leads to the kingdom of God. Rather the kingdom of shalom is reached *via* the way of shalom. There are two points at which political theology is appealing. First, the call for justice is undoubtedly central to an understanding of the Christian mission. Second, the eschatological framework for present orthopraxis provides a measure of hope and vitality to the sometimes discouraging experiments in the present. However what has been all but abandoned in Moltmann's description is the way of Jesus.[1] If the event of the cross of Jesus Christ is normative for the way of the followers of Jesus, then we cannot bypass the manner of his death for our political hermeneutics. Our reference point for Christian responsibility is not first the dialectic between a despicable death and a glorious resurrection, but the actual way in which Jesus bore his cross. He did not take the sword; nor did he permit his disciples to do so. He did not muster an army as those who were zealous for the messianic kingdom in his day might have preferred. Rather, in his way of suffering he showed the way for his followers.

The exemplary character of Christ is not depicted in terms of resistance but in terms of active non-violent service to all. The matter of judging between good and evil in such a way as to cause bloodshed was not Jesus' prerogative: "He committed no sin; no guile was found on his lips; when he was reviled, he did not revile in return; when he suffered, he did not threaten; but he [en]trusted [himself] to him who judges justly" (1 Pet 2:22–23). Nor is confrontation with the calculated risk of the death of the oppressor the way of Jesus' followers: "If when you do right and suffer for it you take it patiently, you have God's approval. For to this you have been called, because Christ also suffered for you, leaving you an example, that you should follow in his steps" (1 Pet 2:20b–21).

It is not at all a question of whether or not to bring the hope of the future kingdom of God into present reality. This must be done. It is not at all a question of whether or not to work as advocates for the oppressed. This is the Christian's calling. It is rather a question of how to follow Jesus Christ's way in the world today. Surely the guidelines for our way are given in Jesus' way.

---

[1] This criticism has been now aptly answered by Moltmann's later book, *The Way of Jesus Christ: Christology in Messianic Dimensions* (Minneapolis: Fortress, 1993) p. 113. Moltmann's discussion on messianic peace (pp. 127–36) is sterling. [Editor Swartley's addition for 2005 reprint].

9

Response to "Political Theology and Political Hermeneutics"

LeRoy Friesen

I would like to take this opportunity to thank our brother for being with us this week. This has been an inspiring experience for me. In fact, I have felt a certain element of doxology running through all we have done together, and for the inspiration and teaching I am very grateful.

I have also appreciated the sequence of topics. It has been interesting to start with St. Martin and begin the discussion there. One of my theories is that there is a kind of "closet Lutheran" in most of us Mennonites, that deep down we have our own two-kingdom theories which, just as surely in ways not totally unlike Luther's, divide reality into two kingdoms, with sometimes the lines falling not very far from where he drew them. Perhaps then, apart from personal participation in the military, we allow the "other realm" to be secular in a way not unlike Lutherans. By beginning with Luther we can better critically assess then our *own* thinking.

Everything that has happened this week in these lectures raises questions, for all of life. But for me it has raised questions particularly in regard to my situation as a Yankee, a male, a white person, a prosperous and relatively secure individual. For me the hard questions focus upon the first world/third world relationship, to use those slightly dubious categories. This analysis of church-world responsibility causes me to experience tensions as a person living here on the side of power. The force of these questions presses upon us and I hope that we can address them more specifically.

Moltmann mentioned that at age 19 he discovered that Auschwitz had taken place; those of us here over 40 or 45 discovered in August of 1945 that something had happened, namely Hiroshima. But today the Hiroshimas and the Auschwitzes are going on also; we get them serialized at 5:30 p.m. and the urgency of living in a world with that kind of information, given the topics we have been struggling with here, is pressing upon me and upon all of us.

The one question that I would like to raise has already been alluded to earlier. It has to do with how we go about building a political theology without drifting away from the crucified God. Is it possible to do political theology in the way in which it has been outlined here and yet remain firmly embedded in the God who abandoned and was abandoned on the cross, the God who reaches out not in raw omnipotence, but in weakness, in self-giving, in sacrifice? This is a question that I direct to liberation theology and political theology in general. That's the more comfortable statement of the two forms of my question because it questions them, rather than ourselves. It questions those who espouse political theology about whether indeed the crucified God serves as a sufficient and appropriate foundation for liberation theology.

I think about the depth and extent of human suffering: of El Salvador, Guatemala, the Philippines, Chicago, and even Elkhart. I think of God in the torture chambers and of God in the malnutrition-ridden child. I think of the suffering God in people who are being systematically disenfranchised, negated and dismissed as persons—image bearers of the suffering God. I think furthermore, as our brother has helped us to see, of God as not only being present in those situations, but of opening himself indeed to all the pain, of all the generations, of all peoples of all times, and somehow taking that pain into herself and transforming it. And then I question whether political theology, as we experience it in our time, grows out of that cross perspective or out of a more triumphal dominating view of the deity.

But as I said, that's the easier half of the question because it's directed primarily out there to someone else. The harder question for me, as a person living in this society with my complicities to situations that cause many of these sufferings, is about this situation that exists in the world, on the one hand, and questions about the church, our ecclesiology and our ethics, on the other. If indeed we follow the suffering, dying, and crucified God, what is the shape of our ecclesiology in relation to the victims of systemic abuse in the world? If we follow the dying God, the one who has forged a tenacious commitment to little people, broken people and unpeople, if we follow that one, what will be the shape of our ethic? I believe we have yet to see the full scope of what it means to be so committed to the other, not merely to one of our own kind, not waiting until after the Rabbis and Confessing Christian pastors are taken away before we respond, but in the fashion of the Master of the universe reaching out now and making the supreme overture to the other, the alien, the stranger, and, indeed, to the enemy.

I wonder too what this means for the content and method of learning here at AMBS—what implications it has for learning theory (praxis?) and epistemology that guides seminary education.

10

Response to "Following Christ in an Age of Nuclear War"

Ted Koontz

I'll speak today largely out of my background as a student of international politics and nuclear war. It won't be surprising to you, therefore, that my comments might be a bit more pessimistic than those of Professor Moltmann. This is also not surprising given the fact that I come out of a Mennonite dualistic tradition which doesn't expect as much of the world as it expects of the church. In any case, let me say something about three convictions which grow out of my experience of studying international politics and nuclear war. These convictions lead to some questions that I'd like to pose for our theological discussion.

Conviction one: we may very well destroy all of human life on earth sometime in the reasonably near future. I don't know whether it will happen. I know it is a real possibility.

Conviction two: "realistic" policies that can make this possible destruction less likely are available for politicians who want to work in the "real" world. There are also policies that can make it more likely. But even the best of these policies, insofar as they still exist politically in the real world in the United States, require the maintenance of some form of nuclear deterrence. They are all far from the kind of Christian norm that Professor Moltmann has been talking about.

Conviction three: international politics will not be changed so that this immoral nuclear threat will go away any time within the foreseeable future. Pacifism, I think, is realism if we are asking how we can avoid the danger of extinction that Jonathan Shell, for example, talks about. But pacifism is the absolute opposite of realism when we look at the question of what is likely to happen and answer that question on the basis of information about the ways nations and peoples do in face behave historically.

Arising out of these perspectives (and no doubt these perspectives are open to question) are some issues which merit our attention and discussion. The possibility of destroying human life raises a question about the shape of Christian hope. Professor Moltmann raised the question: "What can I hope for?" I must say that my confrontation with the possibility of the end of human life on earth has forced me to the view that our hope must be in something/someone that is <u>beyond this earth, this history, and this world</u>. How does a focus on "redeeming the world" come to grips with the fact that this world will end, whether soon through nuclear war, or eventually through the burning out of the sun? Stated directly, what can I hope for when the radiation is falling after a full-scale nuclear attack? I don't believe I would find a hope focused almost exclusively on "redeeming the world" very hopeful in that situation, nor do I now find such a hope very hopeful as I contemplate the real possibility of finding myself in that situation someday. This is not to say that we should not care about the world. We certainly should care about it and seek to redeem it. But we should not rest our hope only on the possibility of redeeming the world, even with God's help. We must, in other words, reject both the unconcern about the *world* (in contrast to individuals) of some within the evangelical or fundamentalist camp and the implicit optimism about prospects for redeeming the world found in much theological liberalism historically and, perhaps, in much current anti-nuclear activism.

A related question is, "what is the source of hope?" For all Christians, of course, the source of hope is God. But there are differences in how one sees God acting and entering into history. Again, I'll simply say confessionally that I've been driven by my study of nuclear war and international politics to see God acting decisively in *dramatic* ways and not simply in ways that grow out of increasing faithfulness, intelligence, or whatever else human beings do in history. Is God working through the Catholic Bishops or through the German churches as they become aware of the problem of nuclear war? I believe that God is working there, but will that acting save us? Is not the image of God raising Christ from the dead in a very dramatic, unexpected way, in a way that has very little to do with the continuity of human action in history, a better image of the way God sometimes works, an image more appropriate for thinking about hope in the context of the nuclear threat? As far as I can see, our basic hope must be rooted finally in a radical divine breaking into history, an inbreaking which changes it completely.

Another question has to do with a point Tom Finger raised. If international politics, and more broadly the world, is not going to be transformed and if one is still committed to taking the way of Jesus seriously as the norm for our lives, then doesn't this require that our focus be primarily on ethics for the church rather than on ethics for the world? Shouldn't our focus be on christianizing church politics, creating an alternative way of living within the church that can model a different way for the world? The point where this connects especially to what Tom said is this: if the call of Christ is a call to a radically different way of life, doesn't it follow that that way of life will only be possible for those who choose to follow that call? Conversely, isn't living the cross way impossible for those who reject or ignore that radical call? This is confirmed for me through my years studying international politics in a secular university context. To speak directly to the issue of nuclear weapons policy, my experience with very bright, well-informed, and morally sensitive students of nuclear deterrence leads me to believe that renouncing nuclear weapons is not a position one comes to on the basis of the best secular wisdom. It does not "make sense." Only on the basis of a radically different perception of reality, revealed most fully in Jesus, can one favor renunciation of nuclear weapons while at the same time facing (rather than ignoring or denying) the grim realities of international politics.

In light of this I wonder if our most basic model for relating to the world should not be one of evangelism. I do not mean that in any narrow sense. Rather, I mean calling persons to become disciples of Jesus in a full sense, to transfer their allegiance and to join a new community. This community attempts to live by and witness to different standards, to create new patterns for human living together which in some degree point to the Kingdom, patterns which are signs to the world of newness breaking in, but patterns which are never fully realized in the new community and which can only be models for the world in a limited sense because the world does and will continue to include persons for whom reality is not defined ultimately by Jesus Christ. In other words, don't we need to take the distinction between church and world seriously in thinking about what we want to say to the world, even on an issue like nuclear policy? And shouldn't the highest priority be given to living in the church by the reality defined for us in Christ and to inviting others to join us in creating that new human community?

But despite the priority on living the new life within the church and the task of evangelism in relating to persons in the world, I am firmly convinced that *part* of our care for the world which God loves should include our speaking directly to crucial questions of public policy. Here I am in full accord with a view that rejects "withdrawal" from the world. But if my initial observations growing out of my study of international politics are correct, particularly my convictions that there are policy options available in the "real" world of American politics which can make nuclear war much more or much less likely—but that abandoning nuclear deterrence is not an option in the "real" world of American politics (because those politics are not and will not be determined by the reality of Jesus), there are some significant implications for the shape of our witness on nuclear policy.

One clear implication is that we cannot expect, and in one sense we should not ask, governments to act on the basis of the ethics of Jesus until we have successfully evangelized "the people" so that they see reality as defined by Jesus. This suggests that we should be rather modest in what we call governments to do. To call them to abandon nuclear weapons is, from the "realistic" point of view, to call them to suicide or to surrender of that which is held most dear. At the same time, the implication of my observation that there are policy options which are "realistic" and which can make a significant difference is that there is a path to which governments can and should be called which is different from the path of full discipleship (the discipleship path being one which can be "seen" only by those who see Jesus as the definition of reality) but a path which may not lead to a nuclear catastrophe.

Thus I am at once more pessimistic than some who seem to believe that a radical reorientation of defense policy may be possible if only I work hard enough and am more optimistic about the possibility of making meaningful, but not transforming, changes in policy directions within the basic framework assumed by most political leaders. I am not certain how all of this relates to Professor Moltmann's perspectives, but I eagerly await his further reflections on these issues.

11

Response to "Following Christ in an Age of Nuclear War"
Thomas N. Finger

Professor Moltmann, your words have moved me very deeply on an intellectual level and on an emotional and personal level as well. That makes it a bit difficult to respond immediately with some well-formulated questions. If I have heard you correctly, you use the traditional just war theory to argue that a just nuclear war is impossible; the nuclear arms race, therefore, is immoral. Further, at the end of your lecture you affirmed that pacifism is the only realistic view of life in the face of the nuclear threat. It may sound as if you have moved from a traditionally Reformed, just war position to the traditional Anabaptist peace position. Perhaps one reason you just received such great applause is because people thought they were celebrating your conversion to our position! (You have to watch it when you come to a Mennonite seminary!)

I want to affirm my great appreciation for these similarities: I rejoice that in many ways the body of Christ, despite its many diversities, seems to be drawing together and moving towards agreements on many of these issues. However, I would like to press a little further some of the issues that you raised—not with the purpose of uncovering discrepancies between us so that we can engage in splitting hairs, but to enable us to think more precisely and deeply about these issues.

In *The Crucified God* you made statements about Jesus which lead, as far as I can see, in the direction of pacifism. You said that Jesus' whole message is based on a "revolution in the concept of God" (p. 142). God, especially as we see him on the cross, rather than being avenging, "takes on himself grief at the contradiction in men and does not angrily suppress this contradiction. God allows himself to be forced out. God suffers, God allows himself to be crucified, is crucified, and in this consummates his unconditional love that is so full of hope" (p. 248). As I understand *The Crucified God,* you see Jesus teaching us human beings that we ought to follow in the way of the cross; we ought to follow in the way of the love of the crucified God. You write that Jesus "denied that human beings . . . had the right to pass judgment and execute vengeance in their own cause" (p. 143). Jesus "did not call upon the poor to revenge themselves upon their exploiters nor on the oppressed to oppress their oppressors. Theologically, this would have been no more than the anticipation of the last judgment according to the law, but not the new righteousness of God which Jesus revealed in the law of grace" (p. 141). Moreover, you go on to say that the message of Jesus certainly had political implications. In Jesus' day there was no politics without religion any more than there was religion without politics.

However, in your 1968 essay, entitled, "God in Revolution," you wrote that "The problem of violence and nonviolence is an illusory problem. There is only the question of the justified and unjustified use of force and the question of whether the means are proportionate to the ends" (*Religion, Revolution and the Future,* p. 143). This sounds to me like a just war statement. It seems to assume that violence is the rule of life; therefore, we cannot really opt for nonviolence. Since we must somehow be engaged in the struggle of violence and counter-violence, the least we can do is to find more humane and limited ways to exercise violence. Today I ask: do I hear you critiquing that second position?

I have always felt that that second position stands in tension, perhaps in contradiction, to what I read in *The Crucified God.* In the essay you said that violence is a fact of life. From that I infer that we must use violence to some degree. Yet in *The Crucified God* you said Jesus—whom you insist, preached and lived a message with political implications—did not use violence. Jesus showed us that it is possible even in this world to live apart from the cycle of violence and counter-violence. Today you said very profoundly that any use of violence draws us into a vicious, unbreakable cycle of retaliation. You very clearly said that we break out of this only by learning to love our enemies in a new way. And you went on to insist that pacifism is the only realistic view of life in the face of nuclear war.

Let me press the question a bit further, though in this way. In limited warfare, such as in a guerilla action, on behalf of peoples who are severely oppressed, might it still be possible to use violence in a way in which means are proportionate to ends, and in which the damage done is greatly outweighed by the good attained? In other words, is the pacifist emphasis which I heard today (and here my terminology may not be entirely adequate) largely *theological;* is it based on the nature of God and the mission and message of Jesus, so that one must be a pacifist in all situations? Or is that pacifism largely *strategic* or *practical:* is it the only sensible, logical way to operate in a world of nuclear war? That is, does your pacifism hold only or primarily in the realm of nuclear war, but permit exceptions in other kinds of situations? That's my main question.

A second question focuses on the extent to which those who live by the way of the cross and the power of the Spirit can expect pacifism (either total pacifism or nuclear pacifism) to apply to those who don't choose to follow this way. In your lecture on "Political Theology and Political Hermeneutics of the Gospel," you said that Christian groups cannot impose their morality on our pluralistic society. Today you said that the traditional Anabaptist way is to make defenselessness, readiness for suffering and martyrdom, a way of life; however, you continued, this is a personal commitment and not a political proposal. The question, I think that all of us have, is: if we are to witness for and live out the message of peace in our society, to what extent can we expect society as a whole to live by these norms? Can we expect society to go along with them? Or should we, as many Mennonite groups have done in the past, withdraw from such political witness because we can't expect society at large to follow this way?

For instance, to take a practical situation. Amidst the threat of nuclear war, with our vision of peace, should we support a nuclear arms limitations treaty, such as SALT III, IV, X, XV, or whatever? Or should we go further and push for reduction of armaments? Or should we go still further and urge unilateral disarmament? I cannot ask for a comprehensive answer here, but perhaps you, by referring to your own situation, can help us think through the implications of the way of the cross which we want to follow. To what extent and in what ways can we attempt to implement this way in a society where certainly not everybody is willing to live without the recourse to means of defense?

12

Review of Moltmann's "Following Jesus Christ in the World Today: Responsibility for the World and Christian Discipleship"

Perry B. Yoder

This volume represents the fruit of a lecture series given by Professor Moltmann in the fall of 1982 at the Associated Mennonite Biblical Seminaries and again at Canadian Mennonite Bible College. The first chapter, a prolegomenon to the lectures, is an account of Moltmann's spiritual and intellectual pilgrimage. Here he relates especially his experiences in a British prisoner of war camp and how it was that he took up theology. He also gives a brief overview of his intellectual development as represented by his major writings. This sets the stage for the following lectures, which are an attempt to begin a dialogue between Moltmann and the Historic Peace Church traditions. For my part, I enter into a discussion of his material with trepidation since I am neither a theologian nor the son of a theologian, but only a Bible scholar to whom the book review editor said, "go, review the book and have it on my desk by September."

The lectures themselves comprise four chapters. The first three present, in turn, three theological options which characterize Christian political attitudes and actions in Europe: Lutheran two-kingdom theology; the confessing church legacy, especially as formulated by Barth; and political theology—the position of Professor Moltmann. The final chapter is an eloquent plea for pacifism in the face of the present preparations for nuclear war. I found these chapters both insightful and helpful in understanding the strengths and weaknesses of the various theological stances characterizing present Christian approaches to politics generally and war particularly.

To what extent the author has adequately described and fairly criticized the first two options I leave to others, more knowledgeable than myself, to discuss. For myself, I was most impressed with his use of Christology as the lodestone in his presentation and evaluation of these positions. Here Jesus' crucifixion and resurrection, representing the quintessence of Christology, were used as a guide both for criticism of other positions and for construction of his own position—political theology. It is to this chapter, where he presents his position, and to the final one, his call for the renunciation of nuclear arms, that I would like to direct my attention in this brief review.

Moltmann begins with a brief discussion of the nature and goals of political theology. He reports that it is a response to secularization and a political critique of the church. Two points are quite clear: First, the church cannot be apolitical. Either consciously or by default the church has social and political influence. Second, a goal of political theology is not "to 'politicize' the church," but "to Christianize the political involvement of Christians" (p. 36). Here, it seems to me, are crucial issues in which we as Mennonites need to enter into dialogue. The tacit Mennonite assumption has been that the church and its mission are apolitical. Long after missionaries have recognized the value of anthropology in order both to mitigate the negative impact of the gospel on another culture and to facilitate authentic, organic acceptance, we still believe that the cup of cold water—relief, rural development, etc.—done from "pure" Christian motives can ignore political contexts and consequences. This is, of course, a head-in-sand position. Political science is to relief and development what anthropology is to missions. We have, however, never quite owned up to confessing the political effects of our actions, either at home or abroad. Indeed, often churches and our relief agency, the Mennonite Central Committee, seem intent on denying either their political relevance or the necessity for their political involvement to change the status quo. Boycotts, demonstrations, and civil disobedience seem unsightly, if not wrong, to many Mennonites. But the church has not spoken clearly and loudly about what policies in South Africa, in Central America, and in the Philippines we are supporting by not ruffling the status quo.

We are now reaping the whirlwind because we have not taken our actual political involvement seriously. Church members leave their church's theology behind (it is apolitical, isn't it?) when they act politically, e.g., vote. In the last election in the U.S., as reported in *The Mennonite Weekly Review,* practically every heavy Mennonite voting area went for Reagan— for a massive military buildup both of nuclear and conventional weapons, and against aid to poor people, educating the underprivileged, teaching school children in their native language. What do you call a people who hold relief sales for MCC but elect officials who will use their tax money to do the opposite? We must ask with Moltmann, what is the orthopraxis of discipleship in our political situation?

The second major fact of political theology discussed by the author is its future orientation, as mentioned in the third lecture. "The new political theology . . . has declared eschatology as its foundation and as the medium of Christian theology." Some of the implications of this statement he explains and elaborates in the remainder of the chapter.

This emphasis leaves me with several questions. First, the word "eschatology" has become such a cliché that it seems unable to say much. Here, if I understand the argument, the emphasis lies on regarding history as open and needing transformation now in anticipation of God's kingdom. Thus eschatology is here the "code word" for a certain view of what should happen in the present based on a particular understanding of history as it is interpreted from an ideal future. Now this notion of an ideal future— the kingdom of God—as the rudder for our understanding of the past and action in the present, raises a serious question for ethics. In the last part of the fourth chapter, ethics is understood to be participating in liberation because this is what Jesus and the kingdom are about. But, ethics is more than a goal—liberation; it also specifies the way to the goal. Whether this type of specificity can be derived from eschatology the lectures do not appear to answer.

Now it is exactly at this point that the Bible apparently diverges from Moltmann's program. In the Bible ethics is normally grounded in the past—what God has already done, rather than in the future—what we conceive that God will do or wants us to do. This notion lies behind typical phrases like, "the indicative precedes the imperative" or "grace and law are linked together," which are used to describe this dominant biblical pattern of human action founded on and responding to the gracious action of God. Thus in Exodus 20, the Ten Commandments are a response to what God has already done, not actions commanded for the sake of a future possessing of the land of Canaan. The past is more than a pointer to the future for which we strive, it is also the basis for our response in the present, which is the harbinger of that future. Thus Christian exhortation to action is based on what God has done. It reflects its source in God's grace and guides us in actions that are consistent with these paradigmatic grace events. Because God liberated and liberates, so also we work toward liberation. But we work for liberation not in just any way, but along a path which reflects and replicates the act of God in Jesus.

It seems to me that it is exactly this perspective that prevents us from adopting a political legalism that says we must earn our own political salvation or present manifestation of God's grace. The future is open; it is not ours to earn.

This leads me to my last comment and question: what is the relevance of the ethical instruction in the New Testament for our peacemaking today? In his last chapter, Moltmann, having discussed various positions taken toward nuclear arms by Christians, interjects the Sermon on the Mount as a judgment on them. He draws on the last anthithesis in Matthew 5 to point to the necessity of love for the enemy. This principle is then applied to the arms race, and is basic to his call for life without armaments. Here is a clear and fundamental appeal to the teachings of Jesus. What is not clear, however, is how this principle of love applied to the arms race between the superpowers is tied into the program of liberation. As outlined at the close of the third chapter, acting ethically is defined as "to participate in the comprehensive process of God's liberation of the world, and to discover our own role in this, according to our calling and abilities." Unfortunately, ethics so grounded in what we conceive to be God's liberation has often been a major motive for "Christian" violence and warfare. Partners with God have felt the need to eradicate the heretic, the oppressor, or the menace of atheistic communism. Confronted with nuclear madness, we turn, appropriately, to the Bible to find guidance for our response. However, the teaching we find there must not be disassociated from its own authentic roots, namely God's grace. This factor needs recognition in our theoretical statements about ethics. Ethical action, including opposition to nuclear arms, then becomes part of a way of life reflecting God's transforming grace which is extended to all in love. The point of this life, as Professor Moltmann so eloquently writes, is to be cooperators with God in liberation. But the point never cancels the means nor the basis.

In summary, Moltmann has given us a very helpful and powerful contribution. It is to be hoped that he will be joined by other influential and articulate spokespersons in opposition to the current nuclear madness.

Part III

Continuing the Dialogue

13

A Response to the Responses

Jürgen Moltmann
(translated by Carol Martin)

I have not forgotten my visits to the Mennonite seminaries in Elkhart, Indiana, and to the Canadian Mennonite Bible College in Winnipeg, Manitoba. The days were filled with lectures and discussions with students and members of the faculties. The nights were filled with thoughts that circled in my head. I came to teach, but I was also taught. I came to give, but I received much, and I am very thankful for this mutual giving and taking. A deep feeling of fellowship with these Mennonite brothers and sisters has grown within me. After my return I did all I could to present and recommend the Mennonite peace witness in the magazines and newspapers of the Evangelical Church in Germany. In the Foreword of my new book on *Politische Theologie—Politische Ethik* (Munich: Chr. Kaiser, 1984) I write: "In the fellowship of this 'peace church' I was encouraged to persevere in this direction: the political peace witness of Christians should be unmistakably clear, and national politics must abstain from military intimidation and the use of force." In the same vein, I would like to try to find answers to the questions raised by the respondents. I am pleased with this further opportunity to work theologically with Mennonite theologians; I trust it is not the last.

The Theology of the Cross and the Way of Jesus

In his lecture, *Tom Finger* explained the most important theological insights of my "Theology of the Cross" very well. He confronted my theology with the "Theology of Anabaptism." Further, he pointed to Mennonite reservations concerning theology and theological theories, noting rather the Mennonite emphasis on the practice of discipleship. As also Helmut Harder emphasizes, this high view of Christian practice comes under the heading, "The Way of Jesus." The "Way" that Jesus walked, and that he showed to us, leads to the "Way of the Cross." Those who follow Jesus are to take up their cross and be ready to give their lives (Mark 8:34-38). The question that Tom Finger asked on behalf of many Mennonite Christians was: What is the relationship between the "Theology of the Cross" and the "Discipleship of the Crucified"? What do Christian theory and praxis mean for each other in view of the crucified Christ? Stated more simply: How are the knowledge of Christ and following Christ to be related in the believer and in the believing community?

The answer from the European theological tradition says: *First* comes knowledge, *then* comes the deed. That is why in theology the *credenda,* or the objects of faith, are dealt with first, then the *agenda,* or objects of Christian ethics. According to this plan, the "Theology of the Cross" comes first, because if one is to come to salvation, one must first and above all recognize God the Father and Jesus the Son of the living God in the Passion and at the cross on Golgotha. Faith is first a "certain knowledge" and then "a wholehearted trusting," says the Heidelberg Catechism, Question 21. This faith leads a person into the fellowship of Christ, and in this fellowship to the "Way of Jesus," and on (in) the Way of Jesus, then to "Discipleship of the Crucified." The strength of this answer lies in the fact that it leads the believing person away from him- or herself and directs his/her attention only to Christ and God. The weakness is that theory is overemphasized and praxis is so undervalued that people could have the impression that deeds in practical living are so dubious and

120

relatively unimportant that salvation depends only upon the right theory or the right attitude.

In contrast, the newer answer from Latin American liberation theology says: *First* comes the Christian praxis and *then* comes the theological knowledge. It is always the praxis that determines the knowledge, not the reverse. Quoting Pascal, Gustavo Gutierrez, in *Theology of Liberation* (Orbis Books, 1973), writes: "Theology is reflection, a critical attitude." First comes duty to love and service. "Theology follows; it is the second step" (p. 11). Gutierrez, completely Catholic in his thinking, is taking love as his point of departure. If love is the praxis, then the job of theology is "reflection on Christian praxis in the light of the Word" (p.13). But if theology reflects praxis in the light of the gospel, then this praxis cannot be the realization of a theory, nor can it be a transferring of knowledge into deed, because it is itself a principle of knowledge. For our question this means: first in discipleship of Jesus I recognize in my own deeds and suffering who Jesus actually is. The strength of this answer lies in the application of faith to the whole person, and therefore to his or her life experience. One does not believe only with the reason or with the feelings of the heart, but with the whole of one's life. The weakness lies in overemphasizing practice so much that one could get the impression that what one believes, or even whether one believes at all, is not so important; it all depends on doing the right thing. The consequence would be an unthinking pragmatism.

A *dogmatic Christianity* without life can easily develop out of the first answer. The second answer can become a *practical Christianity* without faith. Both answers are one-sided. Stated philosophically, the first answer is idealistic and the second materialistic. The truth is not "in the middle," but in a dialectical relationship between theory and praxis in the life of a congregation and of the individuals in the congregation.

The "Theology of the Cross" cannot be subsumed under reflection upon the "Way of the Cross," which one is walking, because in the theology people look not at themselves but at the one who died for them on the cross at Golgotha, and they recognize there the Son of God. But the more they recognize him and the deeper they understand him, the more and deeper they are led on their own "Way of the Cross" and in this way they understand Christ with their whole experience of life. The "Theology of the Cross" develops out of the experiences of and insights into the "Way of the Cross." It is related to this "Way of the Cross," and can never be severed from it. But the theology is not absorbed by the "Way of the Cross," as Christ was not merely a herald to be absorbed in the life of Christians. According to the New Testament, Christ is not only an example; he is first the redeemer. This makes the difference between his cross and the cross that his followers are to take upon themselves: The cross of Christ is vicarious, redemptive suffering for many; the cross we carry is at best a witnessing, apostolic cross. One cannot separate the "Theology of the Cross" from the "Way of the Cross." As merely theory or speculation it becomes blind. But one also cannot declare the "Theology of the Cross of Christ" and the "Way of the Cross of Christians" to be synonymous. As mere praxis, the "Way of the Cross" has nothing more to say and falls dumb. Christo-logy and Christo-praxis belong inseparably together and deepen each other. Both must stand under the motto: First Christ, Christ first!

Because of the urgency of Helmut Harder's question about the meaning of the "Way of Jesus" for theology, I will address his critical question here. In my lectures I examined the theological bases of the ethical and political concepts of the Protestant tradition. I found that (1) the Lutheran two-kingdom teaching springs from a one-sided theology of the cross, i.e., in a Christology that relates the resurrection of Christ exclusively to his cross— as confirmation, as meaning of the cross, or as God's identification with the Crucified—and that (2) the Reformed, Barthian Lordship-of-Christ teaching is based upon a one-sided resurrection theology, i.e., in a Christology of the Pantocrator, who is no longer easily recognizable as the "lamb of God." (3) The newer "political theology" proceeds from the "theology of hope" and understands Jesus as (a) the messianic prophet, (b) the apocalyptic priest, and (c) the eschatological king. With a view to (b) and (c), I have attempted to bring together the elements of truth in the Lutheran and Reformed traditions, as I understand them. I am well aware that I have not yet sufficiently integrated the meaning of the earthly Jesus as the messianic prophet (a). In dialogue with Lutherans and Reformed, one can expect from Mennonite theologians that they will inject the theological meaning of the prophecy of the earthly Jesus and thereby also the call to discipleship in the "Way of Jesus," as, for a start, John Howard Yoder does in his *The Politics of Jesus (Die Politik Jesu—der Weg des Kreuzes,* with a Foreword by Jürgen Moltmann [Maxdorf: Agape,

1981]). I myself have made my contribution to this underdeveloped part of the traditional Christology in my book, *Kirche in der Kraft des Geistes* (Munich: 1975, III, Para. 1 and 2; ET: *The Church in the Power of the Spirit)*. In order not to repeat myself, I would direct the reader to this chapter in answer to Helmut Harder's questions. Here I am concerned with how the message and the way of the earthly Jesus are to be understood.

Jesus' life and his way of living were completely determined by his message: "The Kingdom of God is at hand" and "Blessed are the poor in spirit, for theirs is the Kingdom of heaven." This message is a messianic anticipation, because it makes present the future of God. But because this future of the Kingdom of God is made present to the poor and not to the rich, to the sick and not to the healthy, it calls forth contradiction and opposition and enmity among the rich, the healthy, and the righteous. Jesus experienced opposition from the rich, the healthy, and the righteous from the very beginning. His way from Galilee to Jerusalem had to become a way of Passion. He was crucified by the powerful in Jerusalem. But by God, his father, whose Kingdom he had announced, he was resurrected from the dead, taken up into heaven, and enthroned as Lord of the Kingdom of God. I believe this to be enough evidence for my theory that anticipation and opposition are logically and theologically connected in the [hi]story of Jesus.

We recognize and experience the "Way of Jesus" in the messianic light of his gospel of the Kingdom of God for the poor. We understand the "Way of Jesus" and his messianic message in the eschatological light of his resurrection from the dead and his coming parousia in glory. We are brought into the "Way of Jesus" and experience the fellowship of his suffering and the comfort of his presence when we take up the messianic mission of Jesus and attempt to fulfill it as our own. People who follow Jesus first participate in his mission, and then experience the "Way of Jesus." This is clearly seen in Matt 11:5 and Matt 10:7-8. To the question of the Baptist Jesus replies by pointing to his own mission: "The blind see, the lame walk, lepers become clean, the deaf hear, the dead rise, and the Kingdom of God is preached to the poor." But in Matt 10:7-8 he gives this commission to his disciples: "Go and preach: The Kingdom of God is at hand. Heal the sick, cleanse the lepers, raise the dead, drive the demons out . . ." The mission of the disciples is described by the same messianic promises as the mission of Jesus himself. Only because of this

123

can the "Way of Jesus" become also the "Way of Discipleship" for his followers.

I emphasize that so strongly here because I have the impression that Helmut Harder understands the "Way of Discipleship" in moral terms and makes Jesus an "example" on this way of moral discipleship. If he were to understand it in these terms, it would remind me of the liberal Protestantism of the 19th century, of Immanuel Kant and Albrecht Ritschl, and of my grandfather, who left the church because he thought that morality and a good life were all that were important.

But just as Jesus' way was determined by his messianic message, so is his Sermon on the Mount determined by his making present the Kingdom of God and the messianic era. The Sermon on the Mount is the "messianic Torah," i.e., the Torah of the dawn of the messianic age. This does not mean that the Sermon on the Mount is a messianic utopia. To the contrary: if indeed the Messiah came in the person of Jesus of Nazareth, and if under his preaching the messianic age dawned, then it is only natural to live according to the Sermon on the Mount. In fellowship with the Messiah and in the possibilities and powers that God pours out on all flesh in the messianic age, the Sermon on the Mount is "an easy yoke" and "a light burden."

The messianic message of Jesus leads us therefore to the "Way of Jesus." In first place is the Kingdom of God and his righteousness and his peace; nonviolence is in second place. I do not understand Helmut Harder's somewhat polemical passages on pages at the start of his article. I would say: Jesus calls to the Kingdom of God and to the peace of God, and this is the way of nonviolence. But one cannot well say that this is reversed, because then nobody would agree as to why the "Way of Nonviolence" is supposed to be good, and nobody would find the motivation and the strength to walk this way. Jesus is not primarily concerned with nonviolence but with the peace of God on earth. The only means for testifying to and spreading this peace of God on this violent earth is indeed nonviolence.

Helmut Harder's critical comments seem to originate from the idea that "political theology" has legitimized the movement toward violence, at least toward revolutionary violence (p. 97 bottom). This was admittedly an aspect of the "Theology of Revolution" which developed around Camillo Torres, but it is not part of that "political theology" that Johann Baptist Metz and I developed in Europe. We were concerned that Christian

124

theology, and with it, Christian existence, be led out of the ghetto into which it had been banished by respectable [bourgeois?] society: "religion is private." We desired that Christians walk the "Way of Jesus" not only in their private lives but also in their public, political, and economic lives. That is why we call Christian theology a "political theology." We have criticized political violence from the beginning and have renounced it in the name of Jesus.

I would like to add a remark about Helmut Harder's remarks about "active non-violent service to all" and "resistance." "Non-violent service to all" could at the time of Jesus and can in our day be easily fulfilled by not disrupting the violence of the violent and not even questioning it. Our ecclesiastical charities and the Red Cross offer "non-violent service" to the hungry and wounded, but they question the violent exploitation and starvation of the people of the Third World as little as they question the wars that produced so many wounded. If Jesus had acted in this sense, he would not have died on a Roman cross, the deterrent-punishment for agitators against Roman imperialism, but would have been given a Nobel Peace Prize, had there been any at that time. But he was murdered on a Roman cross. I understand Jesus' message of the peace of the Kingdom of God to be such that his commitment to nonviolence condemned the violence of the political powerholders as godlessness and blasphemy. This is why he was crucified as an agitator against the political powers. If God's Kingdom is the Kingdom of nonviolent peace, then no violent deed can be of God; consequently all of the kingdoms of this world, built upon violence, are predestined to judgment and defeat.

Jesus' Sermon on the Mount stands in the light of the dawning of God's Kingdom and must, to be consistent with the deity of this God, be understood as universal and all-encompassing. It may not be reduced to the life of a believer. It may not be confined to the private life of the peacemakers. The Sermon on the Mount questions this entire godless and violent world and places it under judgment, for it says that the Kingdom of God is coming to redeem the whole creation.

In the Lutheran and Reformed Churches there has been often enough too much accommodation to the violent schemes of this world, i.e., of the nations. In all love, is there not in Mennonite congregations too much withdrawal from this evil world into the familiar circle of believers and peacemakers? I have no right to criticize. I would like to say, however, that the violent world of politics stands in bitter need of attack from the Christian peace witness. For this world is, in spite of all of its violent deeds, God's beloved creation, and God will come into his own in this creation. For the Christian faith there is no dualism, neither the gnostic dualism of the good God versus the bad God, nor the apocalyptic dualism of pious resignation in this hopeless world. The way of Jesus is the measure and the plumbline, not for "our way," as Helmut Harder says, but for the whole of creation, for he is the Son of the God who created heaven and earth.

The Politics of Following Jesus

In this second section I would like first to respond to the different questions and critical remarks concerning praxis which came from the respondents.

Clarence Bauman is completely right about his criticism of Luther's two-kingdoms teaching. What he writes I understand to be support and reinforcement of my criticism. In the life of a Christian the two-kingdoms teaching does not lead to freedom but to schizophrenia. The experiences from the most recent German history are appalling. Unfortunately the Lutheran Churches of the Federal Republic of Germany have learned nothing from them.

But Clarence Bauman addressed one theological point which even Lutheran theologians with the two-kingdom teaching have also raised. If both kingdoms, the spiritual and the worldly, are God's kingdoms, then we must ask whether a split in God himself must be assumed and whether the *Deus absconditus* in the worldly kingdom must be differentiated from the *Deus in Christo revelatus* in the spiritual kingdom or whether we deal with the One God who revealed himself in Christ and whose will consequently is only to be discerned from the preaching of Christ. While conservative Lutherans like Althaus and Elert saw only the *Deus absconditus* at work in the worldly kingdom, theologians from the Luther-renaissance of the 1920s such as Ernst Wolf, Hans Joachim Iwand, and the Swedish theologian Törnvall stressed the unity of the God revealed in Christ. When one emphasizes this, one can still differentiate between the two kingdoms as different areas of life, but one must concede that all depends on the undivided obedience of Christ in both areas, measured by Christ's Sermon on the Mount in personal and in political life. "Christian person" and "worldly person" cannot be differentiated. There are comments in Luther that speak for the first interpretation and there are comments that speak for the second interpretation. This is explained by the simple fact that Luther knew no clearcut two-kingdoms teaching but responded in different ways to different situations. The judge of this issue is not Luther but Jesus Christ, as he is testified to in Scripture.

John Yoder asked me the question on the "principalities and powers" because I said too little about them and repudiated the term "fallen world." He would like to say "that the powers are good creations, and fallen, and coming under the lordship of Christ." I would respond by asking whether he can show me from the Scriptures (1) *when* the powers, (2) *where* the Powers, and (3) *why* the powers "fell"? One must surely dig far into the apocryphal apocalyptic to find the myth of the fall of the angel Lucifer. The original Old Testament traditions know nothing of it. It is true that the so-called Deutero-pauline epistles Ephesians and Colossians speak of the triumph of the resurrected Christ over the powers, but hardly anything is said about their creation and fall into sin. I would not dispute that creatures other than humanity can detach themselves from God and therefore can "fall." But most of what is said about it is pious speculation. The Son of God did not become an angel but a man, in order to save sinful and condemned humanity. For the sake of humanity Christ then conquered the evil powers that only have power over people because the people are sinners and godless. The victory of Christ over the "powers" is no far-away heavenly drama but occurs for the sake of humanity. But there is a problem here between Paul and Deutero-Pauline Ephesians and Colossians: According to Paul, in the end God will destroy "all rulers, principalities and powers" because he will destroy death (1 Cor 15:24–26). Yet according to Ephesians 1:21 the exalted Christ apparently subjugates these powers, so that they must serve him. I find it difficult to reconcile these two statements about the powers. Because of this, I have followed 1 Corinthians. To state it simply, I do not expect a Christian state in the Kingdom of God; I expect no state at all.

John Yoder then lamented the failure of the Confessing Church in Germany after 1945. Why did the Confessing Church not become a "free church"? Why was there a restoration of the old established church in the pre-1933 form? I cannot answer these questions. The leaders of the Confessing Church that I know all complained about the decision of the Synod of Treysa 1945 and considered the path of the Evangelical Church in Germany wrong. But in 1945 they did not have the strength for an alternative. The majority of the young pastors of the Confessing Church had either been killed in the war or were still in prisoner-of-war or concentration camps. The older pastors around Bishop Dibelius could step back into the old established church situation. The Evangelical Church in Germany is no confessing church and has no right to preen this year in the glow of the *Barmen Theological Declaration* of 1934.

I believe that, forty years after the end of the war, we have only one chance to become a true and confessing church of Jesus Christ. It lies in a new building up of congregations "from below," from the many discipleship and peace groups that have already built upon the foundation of the evangelical church in Germany, but which are not represented in the politics and declarations of the Evangelical Church in Germany. Unfortunately we are currently observing the tragedy that the bishops and official representatives of the Evangelical Church in Germany are fighting these groups of renewal in our church in the name of the state. The little Reformed Church to which I belong is taking the path of renewal that it has been working on since 1945, with its unmistakable declarations of peace and with the declaration of the *status confessionis* in the question of the threat and use of "weapons of mass destruction." We have not yet taken the step into the situation of a "free church" in the German sense because we want to take many Christians and congregations of the Evangelical Church on this path with us.

LeRoy Friesen's question is very personal. He expressed what we all feel and what depresses all of us who have been made into accomplices of violent systems and collaborators in systems of injustice. Sometimes, as a Christian in the Federal Republic of Germany I feel like Israel once did during the Babylonian exile, in a position of extreme non-freedom among an unfree people. Simply by existing and living in this country of the "First World" one becomes guilty of the repression and starvation of people in the "Third World." Our "Political Theology" does not drift away from the "crucified God" but in the name of this God wants to call our society from repression to confession and repentance and to solidarity with the poor. What we call "Political Theology" is nothing other than "Christian theology" after Auschwitz, after Hiroshima, and in view of the starving people of the "Third World."

LeRoy Friesen asks: "If indeed we follow the suffering, dying, and crucified God, what is the shape of our ecclesiology in relation to the victims of systematic abuse in the world?" I have often thought about this and have found in reading the New Testament that Jesus again and again directs his disciples' attention to the people (*ochlos*), for whose liberation and redemption he came. Jesus praises the poor, the suffering, and those who hunger for righteousness, because the Kingdom of God will be theirs (Matthew 5). He promises the Kingdom of Heaven to children (Mark 10:14). He calls "the least"—the poor, the naked, the hungry, the prisoners—"my brothers (and sisters)" (Matthew 25). And there is no indication that these people were Christians or believers. There have apparently always been "comrades" in the world outside of the church and without special faith. If the church hears and accepts the message of Jesus about the Kingdom of God, it will have to step into fellowship with these unrecognized comrades: It is the poor, the weak, the powerless, whom nobody can stand. They are not the objects of Christian love. They are the comrades of God and subjects of the fellowship of Christ. They must be recognized and respected as such, before trying to help them. Along these lines I see the necessity first for a new ecclesiology, then for a new ethic.

Tom Finger returned with another question, which also came up in Winnipeg, and which really embarrasses me. It is the question of violence in exceptional situations. My answer reveals my personal dilemma. In 1943 at age 17 I was inducted into the German army. I watched the destruction of my home city Hamburg in the "fire storm" in July, 1943, in which more than 70,000 people died. I survived only as by a miracle. In 1945 I was fortunately taken prisoner by the English. In 1948 I returned to Germany. My generation was pitchforked into the war long after the war was lost; we were to die because Hitler wanted to live a little longer and to make Auschwitz possible. When I returned, I swore two things to myself: (1) Never again war and never again service in a war and (2) if I should ever have the opportunity to eliminate a tyrant and mass murderer like Hitler, I would do it. In this line, I have participated in the peace movements against the arming of West Germany and against nuclear armament and against the stationing of Pershing 2 in West Germany. But I have always simultaneously admired Dietrich Bonhoeffer, who took part in the active resistance to Hitler and who gave his life in that cause. I also have great understanding for the Christians in Nicaragua, who have joined the Sandinista Liberation Front, in order to end the crimes of the dictator Somoza. I know that both of these decisions in a sense contradict a pure ethic of nonviolence. But I would ask my Mennonite friends to comprehend my dilemma from the bitter experiences of my life. I do not represent the "just war" teaching. I also do not advocate a justification of the murder of tyrants. But I know that there are situations in life in which one must resist and become guilty, in order to save human lives. Perhaps Bonhoeffer was right when he spoke of a conscious assumption of guilt in such cases. My generation in Germany became guilty because we did nothing to hinder the mass murder of the Jews. "Auschwitz" remains our mark of Cain.

I want to close with *Ted Koontz's* question, because it asks about hope: "What can I hope for?" I will answer personally: I hope in God and trust myself to the faithfulness of the Lord. He will fulfill his promises and not allow my hope to be destroyed. What does that mean? I hope for eternal life in the Kingdom of the living God. It will come out of eternity into time and out of the "over there" into the present. Because this hope is founded in the resurrection of Christ from the dead, it reaches beyond death and cannot be killed by any death—even atomic death. This is my great and eternal hope. It is the foundation and source of my little and temporal hopes. Because the development of armaments and the incapability of humanity give every reason for pessimism, I set my active hope against them. I am no optimist, but I will not allow myself to be driven into resignation by the threatening world catastrophe. Many people have allowed themselves to lose courage in the face of this danger. My hope for earthly peace and for the survival of humanity and nature on earth is a hope in opposition to despair; I hope *in spite of.* And that is why I believe that politics without the threat of mass destruction is possible. I also believe that abandoning nuclear deterrence is an option in the real world of American politics. That is why I work in the politics of my own country for real steps towards nuclear disarmament and for the building of a non-terrorist world system. It is realistic because it serves life.

It was asked again and again whether the Sermon on the Mount is valid only for believing Christians or also for politics. I am convinced that the Sermon on the Mount is valid for all, because it is the law for the Kingdom of the God who created all people, and who wills that all receive salvation. The Sermon on the Mount was directed to the disciples of Jesus and "to the people" (*ochlos*): "When he saw the people, he went up on the mountain and seated himself, and his disciples came to him, and he taught them" (Matt 5:1). The Sermon on the Mount is valid for the people in America, in Europe, in Russia and Asia, wherever it is heard. It determines the *politics of discipleship* and also *discipleship in politics*.

14

Peacemaking and Dragonslaying in Christianity

Jürgen Moltmann

The Contradiction

Before religious communities can contribute anything to world peace, they must themselves become religions of peace and overcome tendencies in their own traditions to hostility and the destruction of enemies.

"Violence" (*Gewalt*) covers a variety of phenomena. There is the everyday force in interactions between humans and against weaker creatures: violence against children, against women, against people with disabilities, against animals, harassment in offices and workshops. It includes physical brutality, mental cruelty, and much more. I shall limit myself here to the violence involved in the question of "war or peace." I am differentiating between "violence" (*Gewalt*) and "power" (*Macht*).

By *violence* I mean the unjustified use of coercion. We also speak in this sense of "brute force," "lawless force," and "tyranny." By *power* I mean a justifiable threat and use of coercion, legitimized by law and justice. Yet what we understand by power is much more the nonviolent overcoming of conflicts: the power of understanding, the power of reconciliation, the power of love, of healing—in short, the power of life. It is with regard to life itself that violence and power differ. Violence has to do with injury to life, and ultimately always with death. The power of life, however, consists of the enabling of life and affirmation of the forces of life. Power is good— how else could we call God the "Almighty"! Violence is, therefore, a perversion of the power by the impulse toward death. Our main question, then, is this: can the violence of death be converted into the *power* of life?

What does Christianity have to do with power and violence in this sense? If we go into a church—for example, into the Stiftskirche in Tübingen—we hear the gospel of peace and are welcomed and blessed with the peace of God. "Blessed are the peacemakers," says Jesus in the Sermon on the Mount, "they shall be called the children of God" (Matt 5:9). What has Jesus to do with violence? "Put your sword back into its place," he says to Peter. "All who take the sword will perish by the sword" (Matt 26:52). Don't we find the guidelines for a nonviolent life and the work of peace in the Sermon on the Mount? Are not the defenseless child in the crib and the powerless man on the cross both positioned at the center of Christian worship? Can there be a more radical questioning and refusal of any violence in this world than faith in God's presence in Jesus? Or have we overlooked something?

If we then leave the Stiftskirche in Tübingen, we stand in the Holzmarkt in front of a column: it is Saint George, who slays the dragon with his spear. Dragonslayers like this stand in front of all the churches in Christendom that are dedicated to St. George or the Archangel Michael. It is either St. George, who slays the terrestrial dragon, or the Archangel Michael, who annihilates the apocalyptic dragon in the sky—the ancient serpent, Satan, the prince of this world (Rev 12:7-9). In contrast to China, in the West the dragon is the symbolic beast of evil—the one who is repulsively ugly, stinkingly poisonous, and intolerably horrible.[1] In the Holy Roman Empire, from the time of the Christian emperors Theodosius and Justinian, the dragon was declared to be a symbol for the enemies of God and the enemies of the empire. Enemies of the faith are enemies of

---

[1] Uwe Steffen, *Drachenkampf: Der Mythos vom Bösen*, Buchreihe Symbole (Stuttgart: Kreuz, 1984).

the state and are to be killed like dragons. Saint George was transformed from a Christian martyr into a militaristic, imperial saint, and the Archangel Michael was chosen to be the guardian angel of the Holy Roman Empire. The one slays terrestrial evil, the other evil in heaven. They kill mercilessly and with extreme violence. Otto I conquered the heathen Hungarians in 955 on the Lechfeld near Augsburg under the banners of Michael, the heavenly dragonslayer. From the borders of the Holy Roman Empire at Mont Saint Michel in Normandy to Monte San Angelo at Gargano in southern Italy, these were the pilgrimage sites of the *Imperium Christianum*.

How did this contradiction come about—the contradiction between Jesus' message of peace and the Christian dragonslayer in heaven and on earth?

We will first focus on the political theology of the Christian *Imperium Sacrum* and then make the leap into modern times and deal with the monopoly of force in the modern constitutional state and its control through law and justice. Lastly, we will explore possibilities of converting hostile forces into energies for life through the love of enemies.

The Holy Empire

Whatever else may be said historically about the so-called Constantinian turn, it led to the transition from the defenseless, persecuted church to the only "permitted religion" (*religio licita*) in the Roman Empire, but finally to the all-dominating Christian imperial religion. The *Pax Romana*, which began with the emperor Augustus and which the emperor Constantine claimed to complete, became merged with the *Pax Christi*.[2] The Roman Empire assumed the form of the thousand-year-old reign of Christ, which was meant to go to the ends of the earth and last till the end of time. It was no longer Pontius Pilate, under whom Jesus suffered and was crucified, who connected the Christian faith with political power; it was Augustus who, according to Luke's account of the Christmas story, made Jesus a Roman taxpayer through the levying of the first imperial tax. With this, "Rome" lost the anti-God and anti-Christian character

---

[2] Erik Peterson, "Der Monotheismus als politisches Problem [1934]," in idem, *Theologische Traktate,* Hochland Bücherei (Münster: Kösel, 1951) 45–148.

given it in Revelation 13 and became the power in salvation history that was to spread the reign of Christ on earth. From the apocalyptic city developed the "eternal city," which in the benediction *urbi et orbi* has since been declared every year to be the center of the world.

The Christian empire also began with a cross; but it was not the cross of Jesus on Golgotha, but that cross seen in a dream, in the sign of which Constantine triumphed in 312 over his rival Maxentius at the Milvian Bridge: *In hoc signo vinces* ("In this sign you will conquer"). Constantine's cross of victory became the battlefield symbol of the Christian imperium and its propagation. So, for example, Hernando Cortez—with the cross on his flag and this promise of conquering—in 1521 sent his soldiers to storm the Aztec metropolis Tenochtitlan. From its rubble, the Christian Mexico City was built. The Knights of the Teutonic Order, the Knights of St. George, the Knights Templar, and other conquerors carried this cross into heathen lands. It appears on the military medals and flags of all Christian nations: the Iron Cross in Germany, the Victoria Cross in England, the George Cross in Russia, the Cross of the French Legion of Honor, the U.S. Navy Cross, etc. These victors' crosses do not know the Crucified One and have nothing in common with Golgotha—or is that right? Are there not also biblical starting points for this entry of Christianity into political power and the use of military force?

1. The road from persecution to rule is not long. Did not Paul already promise the persecuted Christian: "whoever suffers with Christ will reign with him" (1 Cor 6:2; 2 Tim 2:12)? Thus the marvelous turn of events under Constantine could be interpreted as the turn from martyrdom to the millennium.

2. Does not Jesus' gospel of peace also include apocalyptic judgment speeches? "I came to cast fire upon the earth; and would that it were already kindled! . . . Do you think that I have come to give peace on earth? No, I tell you, but rather division" (Luke 12:49, 51). And still more strongly: "I have not come to bring peace, but a sword" (Matt 10:34b). That is not the short or long sword of the Roman legionnaire, but God's apocalyptic sword of judgment. But what it brings is not peace to those who are separated but the separation of believers from unbelievers.

3. If we look at the future with the God of the defenseless child in the crib and the powerless man on the cross, we see the change from the Crucifixion to the Resurrection, from humiliation to exaltation, and from

135

powerlessness to the almighty power. Did not God exalt him and make him Lord of lords? Has not "all power" been given to him "in heaven and on earth"? Can this lordship of Christ not also take on historical shape in Christian world empires? As we can see in the domes of Byzantine churches, Christus Pantokrator stands above the Christian emperor, who governs autocratically in Christ's name. Thus Christ exercises his lordship through the Christian universal monarchy on earth, and the peoples find their welfare in subjection to this holy rule.[3]

An ancient political theology of the Holy Empire is exemplified from the early period of the Byzantine empire to the Spanish world empire at the beginning of the modern era: this is the so-called Fifth Monarchy.[4] It originates from an interpretation of the image in Daniel 7 that pictures the monarchies in world history: four bestial, violent empires ascend successively from the sea of chaos and devastate the earth with their wickedness. But in the last days, "with the clouds of heaven there came one like a son of man." God gives him "dominion, honor, and kingdom," and all peoples are to serve him. His dominion is everlasting and his kingdom shall not be destroyed (Dan 7:13-14). According to Christian interpretation, the fourth violent kingdom is the Roman Empire, which followed the worldwide empires of Babylon, Persia, and Greece. It is hard "like iron" (2:40) and will "devour, trample, and break into pieces" every country (7:23). According to this interpretation, with the Christianization of the Roman Empire, the final end-time and universal reign of Christ begins. In it "the holy ones of the Most High" will judge the peoples with Christ (Dan 7:22; Rev 20:6). For two thousand years, this political messianism shaped the sense of mission of the Holy Roman Empire and its "apostolic" rulers. Its violence against other nations was legitimated by Daniel's stone: "It will crush and destroy all these kingdoms" (2:44-45).

With regard to this interpretation and its application to Christianity, I should like to remark critically that according to Daniel the empire of the son of man represents the divine alternative to the bestial empires of violence. It comes down from heaven to earth and endures, while the

---

[3] Compare further on this topic, Jan Assmann, *Herrschaft und Heil: Politische Theologie in Altägyptien, Israel und Europa* (Munich: Hanser, 2000).

[4] Mariano Delgado, *Die Metamorphosen des Messianismus in den iberischen Kulturen: Eine religionsgeschichtliche Studie,* Schriftenreihe der Neue Zeitschrift für Missionswissenschaft 34 (Immensee: Neue Zeitschrift für Missionswissenschaft, 1994).

other violent empires arise from chaos, spread chaos, and sink down to chaos. It is qualitatively different from the other empires and can, therefore, not be the "fifth world empire" added on to the others, without betraying its heavenly quality. A Christianity as legal successor of the reign of the Roman emperors and no less violent than them cannot be regarded as the fulfillment of the final promise of peace at the end of history in Daniel 7 and Revelation 20. It cannot be maintained that any world empire is the goal of God's plan of deliverance for the peoples—not the Christian world of progress cherished in the nineteenth century and not the new "American World Order" (*novus ordo seculorum*) of the twenty-first century either.

An indication that the "Constantinian turn" did not lead into the end-time Millennium for all Christians was the considerable growth of monastic Christianity from the fourth century on. With the Christianization of the Roman imperium, what previously had belonged together became separated: on the one hand, worldwide Christianity, which assumed responsibility for the exercise of political power; and on the other, monastic Christianity, which wanted to live in radical discipleship to Christ, free of violence, solely in the power of the Holy Spirit. We will return to this in the last section. But let us now turn in our next move to modern worldwide Christianity and examine its responsibility with regard to power in the modern constitutional state.

The Modern Constitutional State, the Right of Resistance, and the Monopoly of Force

In our civilization, the "innocence of force" of the divine ruler was broken, among other things, by two principles of the Christian tradition:

1. "Render to Caesar what is Caesar's, and to God what is God's." With this wise distinction of Jewish tradition, Jesus split up the theocracy of the ancient world. The political ruler is neither God nor of divine origin, as the last Japanese emperor (*Tenno*) still contended, but human like everyone else. His office entitles him to respect, but he is not due veneration. In its martyrs the church rejected the emperor cult of the Roman Empire and replaced it with intercession for the emperor. In this intercession he appears alongside the poor and the sick, as an especially threatened person, as it were. The separation of the religious from the

political dimension, in the long view, disenchanted, de-demonized, and secularized political force. Hence it follows that the exercise of political power is also subordinate to the judgment of God and must answer to his law. Each act of political power is thereby accountable to justice and law. The old dictatorial principle, "the will of the leader is law" (*auctoritas facit legem*), no longer applies. Only justice authorizes and legitimates the exercise of power. The unjust power of the stronger is still always a reality in human history, but the "right of the stronger" no longer exists. Political power must be exercised legally and legitimately, but if it is arbitrary and exercised with "naked force," it must be resisted in the name of law and justice.

With the separation between "God" and "Caesar," the "religious" state with its uniform religion came to an end. The religious community is no longer responsible for a compulsory state religion that binds the people together (Shinto state). The state becomes religiously neutral and no longer guarantees the rights of only one religion, but rather individual and corporate religious freedom. That does not mean that the religious communities are not permitted to play a role in the democratic decision-making process. On the contrary: like other groups, religions have the right and duty to express their opinion about questions touching the life of the people.

But along with the old political religion, all religious politics come to an end. The modern constitutional state guarantees the freedom of religion and does not interfere in the internal affairs of religious communities. For their part, however, these communities must comply with all the laws in force. There are no special arrangements for them. Child sacrifice, burning of widows, persecuting apostates, and killing nonbelievers are not permissible, but are punished.

2. The second principle originates from the biblical creation story. According to Jewish and Christian tradition, God did not install a ruler as his "image and representative" on earth, but *humans*: "male and female he created them" (Gen 1:27). To be in the image of God—the traditional dignity of the oriental monarch now applies to each woman, each man, and each child, at every age. This anthropological principle has worked in a revolutionary manner until today, and was the basis of the first human rights laid down in the American Declaration of Independence: "We hold these truths to be self-evident that all men are created equal." That is the

democratic principle of equality. If all humans are created equal, then they are equal before the law. If all humans are created equal and free, then governments and political power exist "of the people, by the people, and for the people," as Abraham Lincoln articulated in his unforgettable Gettysburg Address.

And something else is important in this ancient story of creation. Adam and Eve are not understood particularistically as the first Jews and the first Christians, but universally as the first humans. In the myths of many peoples, the first humans are always the tribal fathers and mothers, who came from heaven. In the languages of many peoples there are only words for "friend and enemy," "acquaintance and stranger," "we and the others." According to biblical tradition, however, history begins with humanity as a whole, as God's image on earth. Thus the special identities of Israel and of Christians are related to the same humanity of all peoples and to their common future.

Law and justice have found their contemporary expression in the declarations on human rights (1948, 1966). Today it is clear to everyone that he or she is not only a man or a woman, black or white, German or Chinese, Christian or Muslim, but primarily a human being and thus a member of the human race—and that means with the same inalienable and indestructible individual human rights. It is the acknowledgment and implementation of these human rights for each and every human that will decide today whether the peoples, races, sexes, and religious communities will grow together into a world community or will annihilate each other and together destroy life on this planet. Human rights create peace, and it is only in peace that there is life.

The modern constitutional state is threatened today on two sides: by state abuse of power and terrorism from above, and by privatized terror from the outside. It is protected from these by the right of resistance on one side and by the state's monopoly of power on the other.

In the case of the state's abuse of power, the right of resistance operates on three levels:

a) If the police and military of a country—as is not too rare, for example, in Latin America—break the laws of the state, they must be brought to court to take responsibility. For this the elected government is also responsible. If it does not or cannot do so, then the people and their representatives are not only entitled to resist, but also obligated to do so, in order that law and justice may be established.

b) If a government issues laws that contradict its own constitution, it must be indicted before the constitutional court of the country. If that is not possible, the people and their legal representatives are obligated to resist in order to restore the constitutional order.

c) If a government comes to power through a putsch from within or an external occupation, the right to resist is permitted on all levels. The illegal seizure of power and continual abuse of power count as tyranny or dictatorship. According to the major Christian traditions, passive and active resistance are then mandatory. According to Article 14 of the Reformed *Scottish Confession* of 1560, it is part of the Christian love of neighbor "to resist tyranny, to protect the life of the innocent, and release the oppressed."[5] According to the Lutheran *Augsburg Confession* Article 16, a Christian may only obey the authorities as long as that does not entail sin (*nisi cum peccare jubent*).

Today the law and justice of nations are not only threatened from above by the misuse of power and terror, but also by the privatized terror of criminal organizations, such as has recently been perpetrated by Al Qaida.[6] The great world wars of the twentieth century would seem to have been replaced in the twenty-first century by terrorism against the modern civilized world. Today there is an international market in weapons and violence, where weapons and unemployed mercenaries can be bought. Both of these come mostly from collapsing states, in which the state monopoly of force has broken down. Where states can no longer impose their monopoly of force, privatized force develops, by which whole countries can be intimidated. States have already broken down when the police can no longer venture into the slums of the urban centers at night, and the law of the jungle prevails. Moreover, the state monopoly of force is already undermined when "security" becomes a commodity that only

---

[5] See Karl Barth, *Gifford Lectures Delivered in the University of Aberdeen, in 1937 and 1938,* trans. J. L. M. Haire and Ian Henderson (London: Houghton and Stodder, 1938); Arthur Kaufmann, editor, *Widerstandsrecht,* Wege der Forschung 173 (Darmstadt: Wissenschaftliche Buchgesellschaft, 1972).

[6] Mary Kaldor, *New and Old Wars: Organized Violence in a Global Era* (Stanford: Stanford University Press, 1999); Erhard Eppler, *Vom Gewaltmonopol zum Gewaltmarkt?: Die Privatisierung und Kommerzialisierung der Gewalt* (Frankfurt: Suhrkamp, 2002).

the rich can afford; they withdraw into "gated communities" and hire private security agencies. When it gets to such situations as these, the state monopoly of force has to be defended or restored. Only if the state controls force can force be controlled by law. Without the state's monopoly of power, as I should now like to call it, there is no internal or external security. The common law creates peace.

The battle against privatized terrorist force is internally a task for the police. If this terrorism takes on international dimensions, international police forces have to be organized. If organizations such as Al Qaida attack "the modern world," then the commonwealth of nations must act, as the UN Security Council did on September 13, 2001, after the attacks of September 11. This is no different than the national foreign policy we have known hitherto—that is, the employment of the military for the maintenance of external security, global domestic policy (*Weltinnenpolitik*), already described many years ago by the German physicist and philosopher Carl-Friedrich von Weizsäcker. Then the domestic political tasks of the police coincide with the foreign policy tasks of the military, as is the case with the UN Peacekeeping Forces actions—for example, in the Balkans. In Afghanistan as well, the UN peace missions have taken over military-supported police action.

If global domestic policy (*Weltinnenpolitik*) is the right answer to international organized terrorism, unilateral national forays against terrorist regimes in other countries must be forbidden. Yet the international solidarity in the UN missions has not been very strong. It is understandable—even if unacceptable—that the United States, as the number one military power, should rely more on its own superiority than on the community of the UN. Those who regret this will participate in the build-up of a strong internal global politics, as the way to implement their responsibility for the world. We need the UN's monopoly of force, legitimated by international law. Worldwide Christianity will play its part for peace through justice.

Overcoming Enmity through the Power of Life

In this unredeemed world we need the state, the state monopoly of force, and its commitment to law and justice. External peace can be secured in no other way, and terrorism cannot be suppressed. Yet the state's power is also a phenomenon of this unredeemed world. Therefore we need the complementary abilities to build nonviolent peace in aid of a life that one can love and live gladly together with others. The state can furnish the objective basic conditions for such a peace through police measures and military peacekeeping actions; but it cannot imbue them with life. It cannot change peoples' hearts, nor can it change enemies into friends or good neighbors. Inner peace cannot be achieved by force. Humans must achieve it for themselves. The state is dependent, therefore, on the peace initiatives of non-governmental organizations. A good example is the present situation in Sarajevo: the UN peacekeeping forces secure external peace and prevent the former mortal enemies from attacking each other all over again. The various initiatives like "Doctors without Borders," "Amica," the women's organization, as well as child welfare organizations and interreligious communities, all infuse external peace with new life. There are situations, as in the Balkans, in which a termination of hostilities must create the external conditions for internal peacemaking. There are other situations, as in Israel/Palestine, where these peace groups must lead the way and show the enemies that a common life is possible, despite murder and retaliation.

Peace is, on the one hand, the absence of violence, and on the other, the presence of justice. In the full sense of the word, however, peace is only present where there is life—life together, good life, loved life—to use an ancient word: *Shalom*.

There are two possible ways of dealing with enmity when it has developed and attacks us: *Either* we will become the enemies of our enemies, and attempt to destroy all of our real enemies (as well as all of our potential enemies by preemptive strikes). We then follow the deadly friend/enemy thinking: "Whoever is not for us is against us." *Or* we try to overcome the enmity that has developed and turn our enemies into friends—or at least good neighbors. In that case we must never become the enemies of our enemies, but must recognize the causes of their enmity and attempt to eliminate those causes.

The first way is the way of the violent. The killing fields of history demonstrate its insanity. Because it is insanity, the one who becomes the enemy of his enemies may kill as many enemies as he can, but he always creates new enemies through his own animosity. The result of "friend-enemy thinking" is a world that is hostile in principle. Occasionally one then discovers at the end in exhaustion—if one survives at all—that there is no peace if we become the enemy of our enemies. We must first free ourselves from the enmity, because enmity destroys not only the life of the victim, but also the life of the perpetrator. It is only logical that mass murderers who run amok kill themselves in the end. "Your people love life," the Mullah Omar in Afghanistan is supposed to have said to a western journalist, "but our young people love death." He meant: the death of their enemies and their own deaths.

The Christian tradition provides a beautiful counterimage to St. George the dragonslayer. It is St. Martha. We owe her redisovery to my wife, Elisabeth Moltmann-Wendel.[7] According to the legend, Martha—along with her sister Mary and brother Lazarus—came by ship to southern France and evangelized the Rhone Valley. In Tarascon, she was shown the bloodthirsty dragon, to which young girls had to be sacrificed each year. Martha subdued the monster with holy water, put a leash around its neck, and sent it back to the Mediterranean, in whose depths it was at home. It had only strayed into the Rhone River, had felt lost and had therefore become malicious. Dragonslaying or dragontaming: is one the male and the other the female method of dealing with evil? I believe that men can also turn evil into good. It is not only individuals who have to be redeemed from evil. The criminal energies that have been invested in evil must also be redeemed and turned to good; just swords can be made into plowshares. Out of the violence of killing, the forces of loving can develop.

But how can enmity be overcome and our common life be redeemed from destruction? In the New Testament we have two pointers to the power of redemption from destructive violence:

1. The figure of the "Suffering Servant" endures the hostility in sovereign fashion and does not retaliate. He overcomes the threatening hostility first in himself, then in his enemies. According to Isaiah 53, God himself is present in him in the midst of this hostile world. According to the early Christian witnesses, Jesus brought peace into this violent world "by the blood of his cross" (Col 1:20). "In his flesh he took away the

---

[7] Elisabeth Moltmann-Wendel, *Ein eigener Mensch werden: Frauen um Jesus* (Gütersloher, 2000) 46; ET = *The Women around Jesus*, trans. John Bowden (New York: Continuum, 1982).

enmity" (Eph 2:14). And stronger yet, it is said that he brought "the hostility to an end" (Eph 2:16). That is more than simply patient endurance, and "the wiser one giving way." It is an active passion for life, which is destroyed for both victims and perpetrators through their enmity. When the dying Jesus prayed for his executioners—"Father, forgive them, because they do not know what they do"—he was no longer a pitiable victim, but their sovereign redeemer from sin. It is in the self-surrender of the Crucified One that the power of the life is revealed, not in the Pantokrator who leads Christian potentates to deadly victories over their enemies. For the passion of Christ also reveals the passion of God, God's suffering for life and his readiness to suffer for its preservation. Human acts of violence are always under pressure of time because they have no time. Therefore patience is superior. Forbearance has time and is more powerful.

2. The other pointer to the power of the life is found in the rationale of the requirement to love our enemies in the Sermon on the Mount:

> He makes his sun rise on the evil and on the good, and sends rain on the just and on the unjust. For if you love those who love you, what reward have you? Do not even the tax collectors do the same? (Matt 5:45b-46)

"Sun" and "rain" are not only matriarchal symbols. They are also the material forces for every living thing on the earth. They give life without discrimination to the evil and the good, friends and enemies. Sun and rain are obviously not interested in our conflicts and hostilities, but in our living together. So, too, the love of enemies should overcome hostility and serve the common good.

The hatred of enemies sets in motion the deadly spiral of violence that follows the law of retaliation. The love of enemies plays a different game with the enemy: it is the game of love for the common good.

The first step in the love of enemies is not to allow hostility to be imposed on us by the enemy, but to free ourselves from this obvious compulsion. Our orientation is important for this: We are not the enemies of our enemies. We are "children of our father in heaven," as Jesus calls us. Thus we will not answer hatred with hatred and will not repay our enemies for their misdeeds, but will attempt to correspond to God, who, like the sun and rain, loves life. When we do not react with hostility to hostility, we make it possible for our enemies to forego their hostility and to take up the common good.

The second step in love of our enemies is the recognition of the other. According to Martin Buber's translation, the law of loving one's neighbor reads: "Love your neighbor as yourself, because he is like you." I recognize myself in the other and the other in me. He has the same human dignity and the same human rights that I assume for myself. This recognition of the other is important, because every hostility begins with the dehumanization of enemies; that is, they are subhuman, vermin, weeds, and scoundrels, and they must be exterminated. The normal inhibitions to kill are diminished by such dehumanizations. War can begin. If the U.S. is "the Great Satan" and Israel "the Small Satan," then Americans and Israelis are enemies of God and can be killed, wherever one finds them. Hostility always begins with the vilification of others.

The third step in the love of enemies must lead to a realization of the basis for hostility. Because aggressions develop primarily from injuries suffered, it is helpful to hear the stories of suffering told by hostile individuals or peoples, and together with them to try to find ways of healing these tormenting memories. This requires not an attitude of superior condescension, but compassion, "co-suffering." The location of such meetings is often the mass graves of the other side. The times of such meetings are the shared times of mourning.

The love of enemies does not function purely on an emotional level and only with good intentions. It must also be intelligent, as was said in the peace movement of the 1980s. It proceeds rationally. The love of enemies cannot lead merely to masochistic subjugation under the force of enemies, because then the love of enemies as the determining subject would be lost. The modern hostage syndrome—where hostages identify themselves with terrorists—develops from fear, not out of love. With the rational love of enemies we also strive to protect our enemies from sinking ever deeper into hostility. I imagine this as with one hand warding off aggression, and with the other hand offering peace and a shared life. I do not love my enemies because they are enemies, but because God created them and desires their life, not their self-destruction through hostility.

The love of enemies is also not sentimental, a dispositional ethics, as many advocates of so-called *Realpolitik* (following Max Weber) seem to suppose. The love of enemies is a realistic ethic of responsibility. It requires not only taking responsibility for one's own life and the lives of one's family, but also for the lives of enemies and their families, as the sun shines on the evil and the good and gives life to all.

I close with a story that I heard after World War II. It is the story of a simple Russian woman. She distributed bread to a line of German prisoners-of-war, who were being driven through her village. When the Russian soldiers wanted to forbid her to give the enemies bread, she answered: "I give bread to everyone who is hungry. When the German soldiers drove Russian prisoners-of-war through our village, I gave them something to eat; and when the secret police drive you through our village, I will give you bread as well." That is the love of the enemy which acts like the light of the sun and the power of the rain for our life together.

Appendix

Historical and Contextual Perspectives

Marlin E. Miller and Helmut Harder

Marlin E. Miller and Helmut Harder wrote an Introduction to Occasional Papers No. 4, and Miller also wrote one for No. 8. These Introductions are conjoined here and edited to set the historical context for the original contribution.

—Willard Swartley, editor

Professor Jürgen Moltmann's lectures on "Responsibility for the World and Christian Discipleship," appearing here as *Occasional Papers No. 4* under the title *Following Jesus Christ in the World Today*, point a direction in theological ethics that challenges mainstream Protestant churches to accept the way of Christian discipleship and the Historic Peace Churches to act responsibly in a world threatened by nuclear disaster. Such a direction would reject a social and political quietism, which has sometimes characterized an undivided discipleship shaped by presumed faithfulness to the Sermon on the Mount. Such a direction would reject a political neutrality which has often accompanied traditional just war doctrines assumed to be responsible. It would combine defenselessness and the readiness to suffer with creative efforts for peace in the present world in the light of God's coming kingdom.

Moltmann's theological itinerary begins by reviewing the Lutheran doctrine of the two kingdoms and the reformed vision of Christ's lordship over all of life. The journey continues by turning from the restoration tendencies in German theological and ecclesiastical life during the last three and one-half decades and by turning toward a political theology oriented to the future. The series concludes with a trenchant call to discipleship in an age of nuclear war. Along the way, Moltmann contends that the paths projected by just war, just nuclear war, and the just nuclear armaments perspectives are neither viable nor compatible with the gospel. Living without armaments, proclaiming God's peace, and entering actively into the service of peace constitute the realistic priorities of the Christian churches and theology in a world teetering on the uneasy nuclear balance between the super-powers.

Both mainstream Protestant and Historic Peace Churches will do well to examine carefully Moltmann's case for a third way. Neither can dismiss the intent of this case and simultaneously claim to adequately re-present the gospel of Jesus Christ. Christian discipleship and responsibility for the world do indeed belong together in a nuclear age. Moltmann's case can be improved only by reformulating and reshaping it in terms of a theology and praxis that would strengthen rather than dismiss it.

From the theological perspective of those communities that invited Moltmann to present this series of lectures, both of which are within the Historic Peace Church tradition, suggestions for a mild reformulation and reshaping of Moltmann's theological basis for his direction would proceed along several lines. First, Christology would be more resolutely and thoroughly based upon the gospel record of the earthly way of Jesus. Anabaptist-Mennonite theology has emphasized more the ethical significance of Jesus' life while mainstream Protestant theology, and Moltmann's theology as well, has appealed mainly to the cross and resurrection. As is evident in these lectures, Moltmann is moving toward a recovery of the Sermon on the Mount for ethics. Is this an indication that for Moltmann and for the Reformed tradition that Christology as such will find its basis less directly in the dialectic of cross and resurrection, and more directly in the life of Jesus that shows how the good news of reconciliation and defenselessness was carried along an earthly pathway to its culmination in the cross?

Second, there would be the tendency to be more careful to protect a certain distinction between the church and political orders, between what one can hope for the church and what one can hope for the world. This tendency has admittedly at times spread an unfruitful quietism among peace church adherents. Yet this need not be. A clarity regarding our separateness can also provide a basis for a faithful witness. While the final eschatological vision of the kingdom of God may not differ essentially, the Historic Peace Churches have traditionally placed greater emphasis than is apparent in Moltmann's statement upon the identifiable people of God, the church, as the viable sacrament and instrument of Christian peace and hope.

It should be emphasized in conclusion that our meeting with Moltmann under the rubric of this lecture series in Elkhart and in Winnipeg provided the occasion for a discovery of mutual Christian companionship. While it is evident that the theological journey of the Historic Peace Churches began at a different place than did the Lutheran and Reformed tradition from which Moltmann comes, it is now clear that our paths have crossed and that we share a common goal for the Christian pilgrimage—the peaceable kingdom.

Miller's Second Introduction

Two years ago Professor Jürgen Moltmann gave four lectures on "Following Jesus Christ in the World Today: Responsibility for the World and Christian Discipleship" at the Associated Mennonite Biblical Seminaries and Canadian Mennonite Bible College.

In consultation with Professor Moltmann, AMBS organized the original series in dialogical format. Two persons responded to each lecture, thus initiating broader discussion. Roman Catholic and Lutheran as well as Mennonite theologians participated in the 1982 Elkhart series. Several of the Mennonite responses appear in this book. The Bauman article recapitulated several issues related to Moltmann's second lecture on Luther; Yoder's comments addressed two questions to Moltmann's lecture on Barth;

the Friesen summary focused several points in his third lecture on political theology; and the Koontz and Finger responses sharpened challenges to the fourth lecture, which proposes an ethic of discipleship for the nuclear age. In addition, Helmut Harder from CMBC contributed a critique of the third lecture.

Professor Moltmann answered these queries and comments in piecemeal fashion during the discussion periods in the lecture series. He also graciously agreed to write a more systematic response to the responses, included as the final article. In its own way, the response to the responses may well evoke further dialogue. Rendering these elements of conversation accessible to a broader readership invites others to participate in this discussion of what it means to follow Jesus Christ in a time overshadowed by nuclear violence.

The introductory article on "Moltmann's Theology of the Cross" by Thomas Finger was given originally as an introductory lecture to Moltmann's theology for AMBS students prior to the lecture series. It summarizes and seeks to evaluate several aspects of Moltmann's theology that may resemble "anabaptist" theological perspectives. It also suggests ways in which both might learn from and be corrected by the other. The lecture thus serves well as a preliminary study to the essays collected here.

In his response, Moltmann expresses the hope that this theological conversation might continue. His response to the responses provides ample challenge to further discussion, not simply as a debate between "reformed" and "Mennonite" theologians, but as a matter of discerning a fitting vision of knowing and following Christ. The challenges range from the relation between believing and doing to our readiness to have our existential decisions judged and transformed by the living Jesus Christ.

Moltmann couches the relation between believing and doing in terms shaped by a dialectic of traditional Protestant and liberation theology. He appropriately challenges theologians of an Anabaptist persuasion to articulate a theological ethic that does not fall into the traps of Protestant liberalism. Whether that would best adopt the dialectic between a preoccupation with right beliefs and right praxis remains nonetheless a fundamental theo-ethical issue and a challenge to further debate.

Similarly, Moltmann implicitly challenges pacifist Christians to resist evil, even if that may mean in extreme cases that one "becomes guilty in order to save human lives." Those whom he challenges may also wish to encourage him to review Bonhoeffer's way of resisting Hitler in the light of Jesus' "resistance" to the tyrants of his time. All will doubtless agree that a "new" ecclesiology and then a "new" ethic are needed. Perhaps this ecclesiology and ethic constitute the subject of the ongoing dialogue. Perhaps the pastoral model of an André Trocmé and the Christians of Le Chambon point to an alternative to the apparent impasse between an approach inspired by Bonhoeffer and the image of silent withdrawal that haunts the European "peace church" tradition during the *Third Reich*.